SAILPLANES & SOARING

Edward R. Plonski
R. F. D. #1
Alstead, N. H. 03602
Call: (603) 835-6920

SAILPLANES & SOARING

the beginner's lift into discovering the wonders and world of silent flight

By James E. Mrazek

HAWTHORN BOOKS, INC.
Publishers/New York

SAILPLANES AND SOARING

Library of Congress Catalog Card Number: 75-10425
ISBN: 0-8015-6512-X

1 2 3 4 5 6 7 8 9 10

Published by arrangement with Stackpole Books.

To my granddaughter, Terri

Contents

7

chapter 1

Exhilaration of Soaring

SOARING IS A superlative sport. None can help but marvel watching a sailplane as it pivots about its wing tip, then levels out and sweeps in effortless silent flight, seemingly disdainful of gravity and oblivious to all that transpires below. Effortless and sublimely graceful though it appears, soaring pits the sailplane pilot against the elements whose endless variety make every encounter a new experience. A day of soaring is never dull.

Soaring is great fun. It is in the true sense an outdoor sport. While it is best a sunshine sport, it also comes close to being an all-weather, year-around sport. Soaring's avid devotees can be seen aloft over snow covered mountains as well as high above hot, scarred arid lands in the West. When winter clouds hang low over the northern United States, soaring enthusiasts from those states escape to the cloudless skies of the Southwest to hunt the elusive thermal.

It would be hard to argue that there is—anywhere in the world—a more treasurable quantity of soaring acreage than the harsh and barren terrain comprising the vast Mojave Desert region of Southern California. Perhaps the thermals may boom a shade fiercer in South Africa and possibly the mountain waves rebound to even greater heights at Colorado Springs, but only the Mojave can boast so many different types of wildly vigorous lifting winds.

The remarkable significance of the Mojave Desert is that its outskirts happen to lie less than 50 air miles from the heart of one of the world's biggest metropolitan areas. As a result, the soaring sites in the Mojave are potentially available to literally millions of the sports-oriented folk in and around Los Angeles.

Not all travel that far in search of soaring weather. If the weather is not suitable near one's home, it most likely will be good for soaring at another site not too many miles distant. There is little problem in hitching the trailer containing the sailplane to the family car and driving to better weather an hour or so away. Furthermore, there is hardly a sport in which it is possible to be lifted so quickly from the boredom of job and humdrum of life with so surprisingly little effort.

SOARING—AN UNCLUTTERED SPORT

In a period in history when there is growing concern about

nature's ability to survive because of the depredations of man, it is good to know that soaring causes no ecological problems.

This is not true in other forms of recreation. The overuse of parks and facilities by hikers, campers and hunters is making them deteriorate rapidly. Nature is unable to recoup from the population onslaught. Lakes and streams are over fished, countless boots are eroding trails and refuse clutters the fields and streams. In some areas winds cannot carry away the pollution from thousands of campfires.

Hikers find that overnight camping is fraught with uncertainty. Many a tired hiker has found to his dismay, when he arrives at his projected campsite after a day's hike, it is filled to capacity.

Soaring, in contrast to the problems hitting other recreational sports remains, and will remain a relatively uncluttered sport. It offers many things people seek in other sports, the wide outdoors, companionship, sunshine, and yet soaring centers are pleasantly free of large gatherings. A pilot especially, is fortunate. Away from metropolitan areas he can often soar for hours in limitless, lonesome sky, and if he sees another aircraft in the sky, it is miles away.

LEARNING THROUGH DOING

Soaring is a cooperative sport filled with camaraderie. It is a family sport for some, a participant sport, a sunshine sport and a picnic sport. Participants, families or visitors, baskets in arm, spread checkered cloths over the turf bordering the take-off strip. They spend relaxed, active afternoons picnicking, helping in rolling a sailplane to a parking area after it lands, or just sitting absorbed in

Away from metropolitan areas one can soar for hours in limitless, lonesome sky. . .

watching takeoffs and gazing skyward at sailplanes lazily maneuvering against the blue.

More and more executives, doctors—men from other professions find the sport appealing. Curiously, many captain-pilots of America's enormous jets find soaring a most relaxing hobby. And many power pilots turn to this form of aviation.

One of the advantages of cross-country sailplaning for power plane pilots is that it teaches how to deal with the kind of air they normally avoid: turbulent air. All air is in motion, to some extent, but the kind that the sailplaner seeks out is the updraft. It is usually invisible, so he must come to recognize its presence by the prevailing atmospheric and geophysical conditions. His power source is the air itself; he must become adept at finding lift and avoiding sink and this kind of education can be of enormous value to power pilots, whether they fly in flat or mountainous country. It sharpens their flying techniques and teaches them more about the sky, deftly feeling its shifting elements through the sailplane's sensitive controls.

Soaring need not be an expensive sport. The cost of taking lessons is the biggest investment most participants make. Even this cost can be held to about $150.00, perhaps less, if they are taken through a club.

The beauty of soaring instruction philosophy is that learning comes through doing. This means the student does most of the flying right from the start with the instructor rendering help only as necessary. Students thus enjoy the immediate rewards of the sport from the first and while learning. Few other sports offer this opportunity.

Soaring requires dexterity and skill. The surprising thing is that almost anyone can learn to develop them. It is different from many other sports in that those who wish to soar are required to learn through the guiding hand of an instructor. In learning to ski an instructor is nice to have, but not necessary. In soaring an instructor is a must. This is good for the beginner. It is good for the sport. It is the only safe way to learn how to soar and to keep soaring safely.

A SPORT FOR ALL

Soaring is a sport for all. It is not uncommon to see a senior citizen climbing from the cockpit of a newly landed sailplane. Surprisingly, a qualified youngster of 14 can get a student glider pilot certificate two years earlier than required for a rating to fly powered planes or to get an automobile driver's license in most states.

The sport beckons to women. It does not require muscle. Rather it calls for intuition, sensitivity and dexterity, qualities that make it about the only sport in existence in which women can compete with men on an equal footing. Hanna Reitsch, a diminutive German aviatrix and soaring pioneer, winner of many records in the 1930's, went on to test-pilot many of Germany's giant transport gliders of World War II and towards the end of the war even test-piloted the prototype of the V-1 glide bomb.

SOARING IN EUROPE

Russian women have long provided a substantial portion of all that nation's soaring and glider pilots for more than 50 years. The United States claims 80 qualified women soaring pilots in 1972. Czechoslovakia, on the other hand, with only one-twentieth the population of the United States has four times the number of women soaring pilots.

Soaring is an international sport especially popular in Europe.

In Germany its popularity dates to the 1930's. Soaring enabled the German leaders to get around the crippling restrictions the treaty of Versailles imposed on German aviation at the end of World War I. Since it is a sport and involved neither military training nor the manufacture of military aircraft, the Germans vented their enthusiasm for flying by going into soaring. At the time, few realized the Germans were also to use it to masquerade the development of the future German *Luftwaffe*.

Herman Goering, who was to head Hitler's *Luftwaffe*

during World War II, in perhaps an unguarded moment, revealed the direction of the German soaring program to America's World War I ace Captain Eddie Rickenbacker in 1922. He said that air power was going to recapture the German empire and the first step towards this bold objective was to teach gliding as a sport to all young men.

Through the 1920's and into World War II the German government strongly backed research in gliding and soaring and organized a vast program of training for the nation's youth. Nazi Germany entered World War II with a pool of 120,000 pilots experienced in soaring and gliding from which the *Luftwaffe* drew many of its combat-glider, fighter and bomber pilots.

Significantly, ten assault gliders carrying 78 glidermen transformed war, when they surprised and captured the presumably impregnable Belgian Fort Eben Emael garrisoned by ten times their number, on May 10, 1940, the opening day of the war in the West.

Soaring has been popular in the Soviet Union since the mid-1920's. By the late 1930's the art and technique had advanced so rapidly that it caught up with that in Germany. However, the Soviet Government now appears to have deemphasized its interest in the sport although the sport continues to have an enthusiastic following. Flying clubs operate in most large cities and outlying regions in each of the Soviet Republics.

Gradually, the Soviet government has tightened its regulation of the sport and now controls soaring more closely than any other nation. Although the minimum age is 18 and the sport is open to all, entrance into its ranks is no easy matter. Before an applicant can begin training he has to take a very thorough physical examination and his suitability to participate in the sport must be confirmed by a special medical commission.

Flying clubs train candidates who must take many hours of theoretical work before flying. During ground training, instructors teach the trainees step-by-step procedures for flight, the specifics of towed flight and free gliding and how to make landing calculations. The ground training completed, the candidate must pass tests in the basic subjects—the theory and technique of flight, meteorology and navigation. Only those who make good or excellent test marks are allowed to begin dual instruction. This rule is most strictly observed.

Flying techniques are mastered gradually. In the first year emphasis is on learning to bank. The winch launch is used exclusively during this year. In the next year the intricacies of tow launching by airplane are taught. Only after an intensive second year is independent soaring permitted.

Instruction and the use of club equipment is free. Initiation fees and other costs are incredibly low in the USSR.

Soaring is very popular in the United Kingdom where there are many clubs whose charters date back to the early 1920's. The British Isles boast many world-famous soaring sites. The development of the sport in the Commonwealth nations closely paralleled its progress in Great Britain with the result that some of the world's most advanced soaring is taking place in India, Australia and New Zealand. Canada prides itself on having some of the foremost wave soaring in the world at sites in the towering Rockies.

Since World War II the sport has spread world-wide. International competitions are held every two years while most large nations hold yearly contests.

Not unusual in scope was the 1972 World Soaring Championship at Vrsac, Yugoslavia, a soaring center since 1936. One hundred thousand witnessed the contests. Twenty-eight countries sent pilots to compete. Yugoslavia now trains soaring students from Burma, India, Turkey, Greece and Egypt at Vrsac.

Thousands of soaring pilots flock to Austria and Switzerland yearly where they ride the countless lifting currents above the Alps. Ideal soaring conditions in many parts of Iran and a national enthusiasm for flying are the basis for a strong soaring movement in that nation.

FIRST STEPS

Soaring is a wonderful sport and a lot of fun but, like everything else, it should be carefully investigated before one makes extensive commitments to it in time and money. The following pages will introduce the novice pilot and any soaring aspirant to the essentials he will encounter in learning more about the sport and will serve as a handy reference guide while in training.

chapter 2

Learning About Soaring

IT WILL PAY a budding soaring enthusiast to learn as much about the sport as possible before starting to take soaring instruction. In the long run this will save time, money, and perhaps forestall disappointment. Too frequently novices drop a sport because, to their dismay, it does not fit their life style or satisfy their physical or emotional needs, or possibly because it demanded more than they were prepared to give.

Soaring is such a grand sport, it offers so much, that it would be a shame if from inadequate advance awareness of some aspect of the sport, one later felt compelled to drop it or lost his enthusiasm—particularly after investing substantial time and money in a number of soaring lessons.

SOARING AS A SPORT

There is a lot of confusion about what soaring is. Many think soaring and gliding are the same. Also, unfortunately, the terms are used interchangeably, even by professionals. This should not be, for there is an important difference between the two techniques of flight.

To clear up the difference between the two, it will help to go back to just after the turn of the century, when man began motorless flights in earnest. Those who experimented with the motorless flight usually built their own craft. Some of the contraptions were quite primitive, others were craftsmanlike works with delicately-ribbed, almost transparent wings. Usually, the designer-builder piloted the craft, for none but he knew exactly how it was meant to fly! He usually flew suspended by his elbows midway in the length of the wing, feet dangling beneath. He got into the air by running down the slope of a hill into the wind.

Once aloft, he steered by shifting his feet and shoulders to one side or the other to obtain the desired direction, much like pilots do in the sport of kite gliding now becoming popular in parts of the country. Since the launch was down hill, these craft did manage to travel through the air in gliding flight from seconds to minutes until gravity pulled them to the earth. These early craft quickly took the name "gliders," and logically so, since they moved through the air by steadily gliding downward through it.

As time went on, enterprising inventors designed and built gliders they could maneuver in the air by "warping," that is, bending a part of the wing with hands or feet to control the direction of flight. These craft were still primitive, did not get to high altitudes, stayed in the air only a matter of minutes, and were not highly maneuverable.

Gliders were soon built that had improved aerodynamic characteristics; and their pilots could get not only longer glides, but also sometimes lift, which enabled them to explore the sky better. Soon some were using winds that had been directed upward by ridges and mountains to lift them through the sky, much like sailors use winds to propel sailboats over the water. For a time this method of flying was known as "sailflying" and "sailing" the skies. The gliders that enabled pilots to do this came to be called sailplanes, and with these craft the historical effort of man to emulate the majestically graceful soaring of the eagle had finally come to pass. While the craft retained the name sailplane, its devotees gave the new art the name of soaring, in keeping with the name given to the age-old use of the winds by soaring birds.

NEW APPROACH REQUIRED

Sailplanes soon startled the world. Soaring pilots began leap-frogging over the sky's shifting, uncharted roadways. In 1930 a German, Rudolph Hirth, flew a distance of 100 miles without coming in for a landing. Sailplanes soared to 7,000 feet altitude, then to a phenomenal 18,000 feet using only the power inherent in the sky. They were intruding deeply into the domain of the airplane. Governments began stepping in to regulate the use of airspace by all aircraft, including the motorless sailplane. Almost anyone could glide without much preparation or instruction. But soaring was something else. It took skill. Skill had to be carefully nurtured by qualified instructors.

Schools, clubs and private instructors appeared to handle the growing number of soaring enthusiasts and to train them for safe and worthwhile soaring flight. Today the professional soaring instructor has become a necessary and desirable adjunct to the learning process for those who want to soar.

The beginning mountain climber can read some good books about mountain climbing, pick a good-sized hill nearby, practice some techniques and have a safe, enjoyable and rewarding first-time experience. Not so with persons bitten by the soaring bug. Books can give a good idea of what to do and what to expect in controlling a sailplane in flight, but nothing but instruction can transmit into the fingers, feet and eyes of a novice, the moment-to-moment responses he must make from the time the tow plane first tugs at the sailplane in take-off, through release, soaring flight, the search for the thermal or wind, and final approach and landing.

GETTING INFORMATION

It may be difficult to get information about soaring, particularly as to the location of close-by soaring centers. A search of sources in the local library may help, although it is surprising how few current soaring books there are on library shelves. Several encyclopedias carry informative articles on the subject.

Another suggestion is to get to a meeting of the local soaring club, or one held at a nearby soaring center. Even doing this may prove somewhat of a task, however. Do not expect the telephone directory to be much help. Most soaring clubs do not have their own telephones. Many soaring schools are small and informal; few are listed in directories.

A good way to find where the nearest soaring center is and perhaps even get some information about local soaring clubs is to telephone the nearest airport. Ask for the operations office, if there is no airport information office. One of these sources may be able to give information as to where the nearest soaring site is and may even be able to provide a telephone number to call.

In addition, most soaring facilities do not have a manned telephone, particularly on week days, and a lot of them have no telephone at all. It will take a trip to the soaring facility itself to get first-hand information about the sport.

THE SOARING SOCIETY OF AMERICA

Probably realizing the shortage of materials about soaring, the Soaring Society of America (SSA) has put together a soaring information kit that will prove very helpful to the novice. To obtain it, send $1.00 to:

> SOARING SOCIETY OF AMERICA
> P.O. Box 66071
> Los Angeles, California 90066

The Society sends a sample issue of their *Soaring* magazine, which is published monthly, a helpful booklet *Soaring in America* and the addresses of local schools and clubs, as well as other helpful information. It is a good idea for those interested in soaring to join the Society, as it welcomes anyone interested in the art, the science or the sport of motorless flight. Membership is $15.00, but it offers a special rate of $7.00 to students who are not over 22 and who are enrolled as full-time academic students. All members automatically receive *Soaring* magazine each month for the year the membership is in effect.

Most nations in which soaring is popular boast of organizations comparable to the SSA, where information and services can be obtained.

THE INTRODUCTORY FLIGHT

There is no better way to get an introduction to the sport and to find and experience the exhilaration it provides than to take a flight in a sailplane. The introductory flight is particularly recommended before making the final commitment to take lessons or joining a soaring club. Many soaring schools give flights to potential students at no cost or a nominal fee, at most.

Take a flight at a soaring school if at all possible. In this way there is no obligation to the club, and it forestalls the need to make any payments towards a club membership before really having had the opportunity to decide whether or not to take up soaring seriously.

The flight will most likely be in a Schweizer Glider Sailplane (SGS) 2-33, since it is used extensively in the U.S. as a trainer. The "2" means it seats two, the "33" is the model. It will have dual controls, that is, controls for both the pilot and the passenger. The pilot sits in the rear seat. After signing up for the flight, the pilot takes over. He is apt to be a brisk, affable person in khaki shorts, sneakers and the omnipresent sun glasses—maybe a commercial or Navy pilot in professional life. He chats casually, asking about previous flying experience and the kinds of aircraft used. Cross the runway with him to the SGS 2-33 resting on one wing in the sort of skewed way, which is the perfectly normal attitude of a parked sailplane.

Step in carefully over the side and settle into the beaten-looking, red vinyl seat that is padded at the sides and fits unusually snugly about the body. Prominent is the control stick, which protrudes up from the floor between the knees. Feet come naturally to rest on two light-alloy pedals. The instrument panel is an easy arm's reach away. The chief line operator comes over and helps to adjust and tighten the lap and shoulder belt and then snaps the buckles closed.

The sailplane will be towed to an altitude of 2,000 or 3,000, feet, where it will be released to soar for from ten to fifteen minutes, depending on flight conditions. It may even be that the pilot will turn over the controls to his passenger for a try at some simple maneuvers. The latter, however, may keep his hands and feet lightly on the controls during the flight even though he is not operating them.

SCHOOLS AND CLUBS

Unlike almost all other sports, soaring is not a learn-it-yourself, and never a completely do-it-yourself activity. All entering the sport, even the licensed airplane pilot, must have a minimum of a Glider Pilot rating before being qualified to fly alone (solo) in a sailplane on recreational flights.

Any of the ratings can be gained by taking a course of instruction given by a certificated glider instructor. This should dim no one's enthusiasm for the sport, however.

Soaring instructors have a philosophy that learning comes through doing. It is customary that beginning right with the first instructional flight, the instructor lets the student take the controls and do a few easy maneuvers. Before long, the student is doing 90 percent of the flying and enjoying the experience as much as if he were soaring alone.

COMMERCIAL SOARING SCHOOLS

More than 85 schools across America teach soaring. They offer two basic courses of interest to the beginner. One is for those with no previous flying experience or those who, although they have flown as a pilot, do not have a license that is current. The other is for the certificated power plane pilot who wants to learn to fly a sailplane.

Most instructors, whether with a school or not, give beginners with no flying license a seven to ten lesson course. Each lesson requires more than one flight, some as many as five, before the instructor feels the student has absorbed what he should in that lesson and has developed the necessary skills.

The certificated power pilot takes a transition course. It gives him the techniques of handling a sailplane efficiently, enables him to get the feeling of motorless flights, the sensations of the various winds and other forces of the atmosphere and the elements of soaring. The course is brief. It usually is a four-day course, spread over a period that makes it convenient for the transitioning student to complete. The average pilot takes between 10 to 20 flights to finish, and four of them are required to be solo.

At many established soaring schools, the course will be well ordered, follow a definite schedule and graduate the student in a prescribed number of weeks. Other soaring schools are not so formal. They take into account the student's availability due to his job or ability to pay. They may spread the training over a year of more. The same holds true for the instruction given by clubs and most private instructors.

Seven lessons give a student a lot of soaring. A single lesson may take several days to complete, depending on the availability of a training sailplane, an instructor, the student's free time or the weather.

The number of flights needed to complete a course for a beginner with no previous flight experience may run from as low as 20 to as high as 45 or more. There are reasons for this. In the Southwest, where there is plenty of landing space, little air traffic and many days of good, calm weather, training can be completed in far less time then in populated areas, where open fields are not available or are hemmed in by trees or fences, or where the atmosphere is changeable. In these latter areas schools wisely require that a student take more training. Thus, those interested in instruction may do well to take it during vacation, heading to an area where it is possible to get a student rating with fewer lessons. While this may guarantee getting the rating early, it will still require flight experience with an instructor from the airfield where the individual expects to fly regularly.

Schools have brochures giving their methods of operations and fees. If the brochure is not clear, question the school's director. Ask if a package rate for instruction is offered. Most package plans include lessons in an instructional, dual-control sailplane, and several solo flights. The package should include the use of the sailplane, the instructor's time and the cost of the tow plane fee. Be certain these items are all included; if not, ask what specifically the costs are for the other items. Get a pencil and paper and add all this up. If it sounds as though it is costing too much, discuss it with the director of the school. Usually, some arrangements can be worked out, time or part-payments so that an enthusiast can go ahead with at least some lessons, until it is financially possible to take more.

THE RIGHT INSTRUCTOR

It is very important to have a good instructor. Giving instruction in the art of soaring is a very skilled undertaking in itself. While there probably is no such thing as a bad instructor, if there is one, he wastes a student's time and money and may even ruin the student's ability to become a really good soaring pilot. The instructor has the job of getting the very best from his student, and the student, on his part, should settle for nothing less.

The student has the right to know what the instructor is planning to teach. Ask the instructor what the course of instruction will be. Get an idea of what the lesson will include each time a flight is taken. However, give the instructor some latitude, should the weather not be what he hoped for, to show or teach a particular maneuver. Should the flight be terminated before completion of a day's instruction because of the weather or insufficient thermals or winds to keep the sailplane aloft, make certain there will be instruction on a following day to make up the period.

Find out if two lessons can be completed on the same day, consecutive days, or whether they must be taken once a week only. Determine which days and what hours.

Schools and clubs have more than one instructor. It is well to make the acquaintance of the staff of instructors before beginning instruction. An instructor has a great responsibility to guide the student in the development of flying techniques, the use of good judgment under varying conditions and in developing and maintaining a healthy and enthusiastic attitude in the student. He should be able to discover any fears, apprehensions or problems arising and dispel them quickly.

Many instructors are pilots who fly some of this nation's largest jets, take up soaring as a relaxing hobby and do instructing on the side. Others are active business men. It could be that because of the demands of their regular jobs, some will not be able to give instruction regularly. This can result in many frustrating delays to a student anxious to get the course under his belt and get into the air on his own.

It is well that the student has an instructor whom he likes. Since instruction may extend over as many as 30 flights and as many as 15 hours, it is also a good idea to find out if the instructor can be available for the duration of the learning phase. Insofar as possible a student should have all his instruction from the same instructor during the pre-solo flying.

The occasion may arise, however, where although the instructor selected may not be available, the sailplane is scheduled and available and the weather ideal. In this event it would probably be a good idea to overlook the "one instructor" policy if some other qualified instructor was available to fill in for the lesson. Before going up, he will study the student's log book and probably ask questions to see what should be covered.

This may actually turn out to a student's advantage. The

newcomer to flying cannot usually judge whether his instructor is any good or not, at least not until he has finally accrued some hours in his log book. But it can become an eye-opening experience at times to have a switch in instructors. Some are, indeed, better instructors than others.

Once a student finds the right school and instructor, he should place his confidence in their procedures. While each school uses procedures different from another school and the same goes for instructors, all do follow lesson plans. No two schools may use the exact same lesson plans, but on the whole, these lessons are fairly uniform and reflect the jelling of a lot of experience over the years. They insure that instruction time concentrates in the most efficient way on progressively building up the student's skills toward complete mastery of the sailplane in any maneuver and situation.

COSTS

The costs of soaring may seem to place the sport out of range for many, but properly understood and budgeted for, they need not be unduly burdensome. As a matter of fact, soaring instruction is hardly more expensive than instruction in sports such as skiing or golf. Beginning skiing, particularly, can be quite expensive on a $250.00, learn-to-ski week in the Rockies. And, the going rate for an hour of instruction by a golf or tennis pro is above $10.00.

In soaring a qualified instructor-soaring pilot friend may give a buddy free instruction. Or, it is possible to obtain instruction free through one of the more than 180 soaring clubs in America. The initiation fee for joining a club, depending on the club, ranges from $100.00 to $200.00, plus payment of either monthly or annual dues.

The practice is growing for clubs to charge $10.00 a month. This covers all costs and means the use of the club's sailplanes at no extra charge, but it does not include tow fees. It could mean that on a slack day at the club airfield it would be possible to soar all afternoon for merely a $3.00 tow fee.

Services and fees in 1972 were averaging as follows:
Rides (Introductory) [$10.00
Instruction (dual for one hour not
   including tow fees) [$7.00
Tow (each, first 1,000 feet altitude) [$3.00
Tow (additional 1,000 feet each) [$2.00
Sailplane rental [$10.00
Courses:
To transition power pilots [$150.00
To novice to reach solo [$250.00
To novice to reach solo (club) [$150.00

Some schools prefer to charge for instruction by the hour only, taking the position that should student interest wane, an obligation or financial commitment should not be a compelling reason for his continuing. These schools maintain that if a student's motivation is high, he will find the financial means to take lessons.

Most schools offer discounts, on blocks of sailplane instruction, time and tow services. One school gives a ten percent discount for $100.00 worth of these services. Thus, a student who has taken a few lessons and wishes to continue taking instruction should investigate available block time arrangements as a way to reduce costs.

It is also important to know what recreational soaring will cost once the instruction is completed. Although rates vary considerably over the United States, on the average one hour of solo flying is $15.00. This includes the rental of the sailplane, but it does not take into consideration the cost of the tow. While this may sound expensive, one hour of soaring gives a lot of flying and fun and is only a small part of the total benefit of the sport. In some clubs the rental fee is as low as $1.00 an hour.

Should the learner be bitten by the bug and desire to own a sailplane, costs can skyrocket unless there is a cooperative ownership. There is also the matter of storing, parking, maintenance and other costs of owning a sailplane to consider. However, these will be discussed in a later chapter.

One final word of advice about costs. For those who want to get instruction behind them quickly and can afford it, the commercial soaring school is recommended.

CLUBS

Every soaring club is different from another. Engineers, doctors, artists, college and high school students, jet-pilots—a variety of people, including a share of non-flyers who like the human and physical surroundings, make up the membership. Many clubs own sailplanes, some may own a tow plane, most have their own instructors. Others boast an airstrip, member-built hanger and club house.

Members are assigned ground duties ranging from simple tasks, such as retrieving the tow rope or running the wing, to jobs requiring more skill and training, including sailplane repairs and winch operation.

Most clubs have a policy calling for candidate members to help around the field doing some of these chores for weeks to months before they can become members. This period of apprenticeship enables members to get to know the prospective members. It also acquaints the candidates with the club, its members, and its customs and requirements and prevents candidates from making hasty decisions about joining the club—decisions which some might later regret.

Through a club it is possible to get instruction merely for the cost of the tow required to get aloft. As pointed out earlier, it is not the fastest way to learn, however. Because of the great popularity of the sport with members, most of the club's sailplanes and tow planes are kept busy. There may be a waiting line for tows aloft, and it becomes difficult for a student to work in his instructional time. Moreover, there is a great deal of informality in operations, scheduling and the like, that can cause a student to become impatient. However, most people who take up soaring in a serious way eventually do join a club—if not for the instruction they may get there, at least for the reasonable costs of the sport, the friendly atmosphere and the comradeship. The wise soarer will look carefully for the facility that offers a pleasant atmosphere and the kind of people he likes to be around.

CERTIFICATES AND AWARDS

A great deal of confusion exists about this topic among new students, as well as those who are new to aviation. It is well to understand the difference between the pilot certificate and the soaring award, in addition to the qualifications for them and who may certify the qualifications.

STUDENT GLIDER PILOT CERTIFICATE

This is an official Federal Aviation Administration (FAA) document. The student must obtain it from an FAA office. It is of no value until certificated by an FAA-rated soaring instructor.

The student must be at least age 14 before he can be certificated. The certificate reads that the student has successfully completed instruction from a rated flight instructor in takeoffs, landings, gliding, turns, stalls and that he has studied appropriate literature. The certifying pilot will not sign the document until he is certain the student has met all of the requirements completely. He indicates in his endorsement any limitation he feels should be placed on the student for the safe operation of the sailplane (such as wearing glasses in flight). He also writes exactly which sailplane or sailplanes the student is qualified to fly.

The certificate allows the student to fly locally. If he desires to fly cross-country, this will take additional training. When the instructor considers the student qualified to fly cross-country safely, he will put an additional endorsement to this effect on the certificate.

SSA AWARDS

Quite a different thing are the awards made through the SSA. The Society is a member of the *Federation Aeronautique Internationale* (FAI) and is authorized to make awards providing certain requirements are met.

A student pilot is eligible for the "A" badge when he has completed his first solo flight. Prior to this he will have

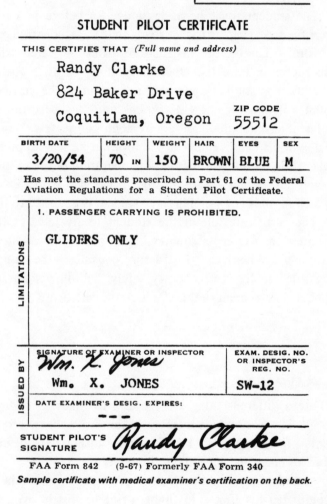

UNITED STATES OF AMERICA
DEPARTMENT OF TRANSPORTATION
FEDERAL AVIATION ADMINISTRATION

CERTIFICATE NO.
ZZ - 04283

STUDENT PILOT CERTIFICATE

THIS CERTIFIES THAT *(Full name and address)*

Randy Clarke

824 Baker Drive

Coquitlam, Oregon   ZIP CODE
55512

BIRTH DATE	HEIGHT	WEIGHT	HAIR	EYES	SEX
3/20/54	70 IN	150	BROWN	BLUE	M

Has met the standards prescribed in Part 61 of the Federal Aviation Regulations for a Student Pilot Certificate.

1. PASSENGER CARRYING IS PROHIBITED.

GLIDERS ONLY

LIMITATIONS

ISSUED BY

SIGNATURE OF EXAMINER OR INSPECTOR
Wm. X. Jones
Wm. X. JONES

EXAM. DESIG. NO.
OR INSPECTOR'S
REG. NO.

SW-12

DATE EXAMINER'S DESIG. EXPIRES:
- - -

STUDENT PILOT'S
SIGNATURE   *Randy Clarke*

FAA Form 842   (9-67) Formerly FAA Form 340

Sample certificate with medical examiner's certification on the back.

become familiar with takeoff signals, pilot responsibilities, cockpit checkouts, takeoffs under varying conditions and demonstrated ability to fly the sailplane alone.

A pilot can apply for the "B" badge when he has demonstrated the ability to soar (climb in altitude during free flight) at least 30 feet after release from 2,000 feet, or 45 feet after release from 3,000 feet. Neither of these re-

The silver "C" pin—one of the higher SSA awards which can be earned through increased soaring proficiency and achievement.

quirements are difficult to achieve and the student may, in fact, build up the necessary background during his instruction to fulfill most all of the requirements for one or more of the Society's awards. Other badges are given to those who have demonstrated the ability to do more advanced and complicated soaring. Awards are made in the form of badges and are sometimes given at informal ceremonies. Most recipients get them by mail.

VALUE OF THE CERTIFICATE

Certificates are recognized internationally and enable the fledgling sailplane pilot to fly at any soaring center in the world.

THE PILOT LOG BOOK

Every student pilot has to have a log book. The student will make some of the entries, the instructor other entries, giving his name, condition of flight, the flight time and other information such as comments about the student's progress on the particular flight. This log book must be kept available for inspection at the request of an FAA inspector.

It is worthwhile spending an extra few minutes writing entries neatly. This will be a permanent record of progress as a student as well as a log of subsequent soaring. Thus, if on a visit to another center or if joining a club, the book will be documentary proof of experience and ability. Do not let an untidy looking log book suggest carelessness or poor flying ability to anyone.

Most soaring centers have log books on hand. If one cannot be located, send to the SSA for a "Glider Pilot's Log Book." The cost is $1.25 and includes postage and handling.

PHYSICAL CHECKUP

If, after considering the several aspects of soaring discussed so far, and after taking at least one introductory flight, a prospective student thinks he might want to take lessons, he should seriously consider taking a physical examination for flying. Actually, the FAA (Federal Aviation Authority) is very lenient about soaring pilots having a physical and require only that ". . . the applicant certify he has no known physical defect that makes him unable to pilot a glider." While this puts the responsibility on the student and the student may feel perfectly fit, it is best to have a qualified physician make the judgment the FAA requires. Preferably go to a certified FAA medical examiner; the county or local medical society will be glad to supply the name of such an examiner closest to the applicant.

These professionals have experience in aviation medicine and regularly examine and certify the physical fitness as required by regulation for pilots of powered aircraft. In the case of a soaring student, the form the examiner uses and certifies is a combined medical and student glider-pilot certificate. When the student has completed his soaring training, his instructor certifies the student for solo flight on the same form.

There are advantages to having a medical examination by an FAA accredited medical examiner over and above the assurance that he is a specialist. One is that the instructor is reassured that his student is physically certified to fly. Another is that this same form, properly certified, serves as a student pilot's license, if the individual should choose to take instruction in flying conventional aircraft.

One should not be overly disappointed if it happens that he turns out to be one of the rare individuals who are told it is best, from the medical standpoint, not to fly. Although it does not happen often, it is not unknown for an instructor to encounter a student exhibiting some strange behavior in the air, which is primarily related to a physical problem. Then the instructor must tell the student he cannot take more lessons. This is always unfortunate, not only because of the great disappointment the student must suffer, but it also means the expenditure of funds towards no useful end. A physical exam in advance of instruction will forestall this.

Nevertheless, if one decides to take instruction without having the physical, at least he should be certain he has no

DATE	No. of Flt.	TYPE OF GLIDER	LICENSE NUMBER	TYPE OF TOW	ALTITUDE RELEASE	ALTITUDE MAX.	LOCATION
5/27	21	S-233	N244IW	AERO	3000	3000	
6/11	22	SCHLEICHR-RHŌNE	N7984	"	"	"	GETTYSBURG
6/11	23	"	"	"	"	"	"
"	24	"	"	"	1M		"
"	25	"	"	"	1M		"
"	26	"	"	"	1M		"

CERTIFIED BY *Mark Volk* 6131615 CFI-G

Sample facing pages—glider pilot's log book.

DUAL TIME		SOLO		REMARKS
HOURS	MINUTES	HOURS	MINUTES	
	31			LESS #5 FLT 21 TOW OK / STALLS OK / NEED WK ON COORD + A/S CONTROL
	20			HIGH TOW, SIDE TOW, SLOW FLIGHT, SPOT LANDING, REVIEW + PRACTICE
	20			SOARING, EMERGENCY PROCEDURE, REVIEW + PRACTICE
	10			PRE SOLO - PATTERN - SLIPS, SPOILER - LANDING
	10			PRE SOLO + EMERGENCY - PATTERN - LANDING
			10	SOLO
				TIME BROUGHT FORWARD
				TOTAL TIME

PILOT'S
SIGNATURE

Sample facing pages—glider pilot's log book. (continued)

problem with vision. If a prospective student wears glasses, he should be certain his prescription is a very recent one, for safe soaring—all flying in fact—depends to a great degree on good vision.

A word about airsickness. Anyone who chronically becomes airsick easily has no business soaring or starting to take lessons. Fortunately airsickness does not seem to be a problem for most soaring students, even those who do have trouble with sea-sickness. The exact reason for this is not known, but perhaps it hinges on the fact that since the pilot is the one controlling the sailplane, he does not feel as helpless as when he is a passenger in a boat. Also there is in soaring a greater feeling of oneness with the sailplane, and a harmony with the elements. There is by contrast less fighting the motion of a sailplane than is the case when one is a passenger on a tossing boat. At any rate, if a student does not know how susceptible he is to airsickness, he soon will know after he has taken an introductory flight. If he is then still uncertain, his second one will most certainly indicate whether he has a tendency toward the problem or not and whether it will jeopardize his soaring aspirations.

FINDING THE RIGHT SOARING FACILITY

There are, in summary, several matters to weigh carefully when making the decision to take up soaring. One should look around a bit before making his final decision on where he will want to do most of his soaring. After all, a large part of having fun depends on the persons with whom one associates. Compatible people make the day that much more enjoyable. A wise soarer will look carefully for the facility that offers a pleasant atmosphere and the kind of people he likes to be around.

chapter 3

A Day at the Airfield

CHECK THE WEATHER before taking off for the airfield, otherwise the trip may be in vain. Is the horizon sharp and distinct? How much wind is forecast? Some days are just not for soaring. A prediction from the weather man of probable showers is enough to cause many schools and clubs to call off soaring for the day. Sometimes, after a heavy rain or the melting snows in the spring, airfields are soggy and make for difficult, if not downright dangerous takeoffs. Thus, even though the sky looks great, soaring may be out of the question because of ground conditions.

Most soaring clubs and schools have a telephone number

to call, where it is possible to find out if soaring activities are to be on or off at their field that day. Some of the larger organizations may even provide a report on general soaring conditions. This number will most likely be that of the home telephone of one of the members. If it takes awhile before an adult member of the household gets to the telephone, be patient! Remember soaring is a sport, and it is very informally run.

It is usually the case that after the would-be soaring pilot gets a little experience, it is possible for him to cock a weather eye at the sky and make a fairly good guess about whether there will be soaring activities on that particular day. However, if the soaring site is some distance away, or if there is any doubt, it is best to verify the day's schedule by phone. This may avoid an otherwise needless trip.

OPERATIONS INFORMAL

Informality is the keynote at the soaring schools or club. No one worries about flight fashions or frets about soaring lounge wear as the fashion-minded "apres" (after) skiing skiers are wont to do. Remember, soaring is an outdoor sport! Most centers are in exposed places and therefore the attire should be suited to the outdoors. In summer, wind chill can make the temperature a lot cooler at the site than expected. If planning to fly, wear headgear of some sort to prevent hair from blowing into the eyes. A cap or beret are best, since they are not easily blown off in the prop wash of an airplane. Some pilots like a cap with a long visor to keep the sun out of the eyes. Others like a beret. It does not sit high on the head like some head covers, such as helmets that may interfere with closing the canopy and tend to bump against it. Moreover, a beret can be tucked in a pocket easily when not needed. Wearing sun glasses is a matter of preference. There is a lot of controversy on this subject, even among flyers. Some contend tinted or polarizing lenses allow one to discern cloud shapes better.

Clothes should be warm enough for the altitude the sailplane is expected to reach. While the novice will not be getting to altitudes where the temperature is below freezing, nonetheless, the higher the altitude, the colder it is. For most local flights, because the cockpit is enclosed, and providing flights are not too long, the same clothes worn in ground activities will suffice during the flight. It depends also on the time of year. If the instructor wants to fly a few thermals and expects to get to a high altitude, a pullover or some other warmer clothing and boots may be necessary. Many pilots keep zippered coveralls handy just for such situations.

Many sites have no hangars, club houses or offices to which one can run to warm up. Even an old-fashioned outhouse is not an uncommon sight at some. If soaring is done at an airport belonging to a fair-sized community, members of the school staff and students and members of clubs may have the use of the airport facilities. At larger airports, expect to find the soaring activities going on in a remote part of the airport away from heavy airplane traffic and the main runway.

ACTIVITY AT THE SITE

The date and weather affect the size of the crowd at the soaring site. Week-ends, especially the long holiday week-ends, seem to draw a lot of sightseers. As far as operations are concerned, do not be surprised if confusion seemingly reigns. In fact, if it does, be reassured. It is actually organized and ordered, particularly in areas that count, such as keeping order at takeoff points, lining up and securing the sailplanes and in enforcing safety. Otherwise, students, members of families, visitors and just plain hangers-on do pretty much what they want.

SAFETY PRECAUTIONS

While the spirit of informality prevails at soaring sites, there are certain rules visitors must observe. All clubs and schools have instructions published for visitors and members that must be read and observed. Look for a copy and read these instructions carefully. One member of the school or club will be on duty as the operations duty officer. Seek him out for the answers to any special questions or information on the day's main events. It is well for a new arrival to ask about specifics: where to park, walk, and the direction from which sailplanes will be coming in to land. Don't take anything for granted. Follow the rules. This may prevent embarrassment or avoid some sharp warning such as is sometimes necessary in a dangerous situation.

Although members' or students' automobiles may be permitted at the launch line, visitors' are not. Visitors must park their cars in the visitors' parking area. At a club, members' cars are frequently used to tow sailplanes to the sailplane parking line or to the hangar after they have landed. Other cars serve as control centers and therefore are allowed on or near the launch line. But these are the main exceptions to the parking rules.

Since sailplanes and tow planes takeoff and land on

Safety considerations encourage a swivel head when in or near the launch/landing area.

grassy areas at many soaring centers, it is a good idea to discover where these landing areas are before walking about very much. When approaching to land, sailplanes make no noise other than a low whistle which can be heard only at close range. Another thing, tow planes often land still trailing the tow line, which usually is about 150-feet long. It is not enough therefore to be sure that the plane has passed, but also that the tow line has, too. Tow lines can also be dangerous at other times. One may be lying on the ground in snake-like fashion between the tail of the tow plane and the nose of the sailplane and appear quite harmless. If one volunteers to help at a takeoff, he must be cautious not to get his foot entwined in a tow-line loop as the plane moves to get into position for take off. As a general rule, it's best to keep one's head on a swivel while anywhere in a launch area.

It is natural, of course, to be curious. No one will usually object if a visitor walks along the sailplane parking line to look them over. However, give parked airplanes a wide berth. Especially, stay away from the front of any airplane and never touch their propeller! Airplanes are dangerous even when parked; propellers have been known to kick over and kill a curious but uncautious visitor.

At well-established schools and club fields, owners will house their sailplanes in the hangar, if there is one. Otherwise, they will be left outdoors. Some owners dismantle their craft and take them home after a day's soaring. This is no problem, since most sailplanes can be taken apart and placed in a trailer, hitched to the family car and towed home to be parked in the back yard or driveway. Others keep their trailers at the airfield and use them only for cross-country flights or when taking the sailplane to a distant soaring site.

One of the most absorbing sights at a field is to see a car and trailer pull up near the launch area, watch the driver get out and unhitch his trailer and then start taking his sailplane out. He gingerly takes out one wing, then the other and finally the fuselage, a task he may do with the help of his wife, or all by himself, even, so light are the sailplane parts. He quickly assembles them and a few minutes later, he may be in the air.

WAITING FOR A TOW

Perhaps the most frustrating part of soaring is the amount of waiting one must do. Whether waiting for takeoff with an instructor, or for a solo flight, this can frequently happen, since often there are not enough tow airplanes to handle all the soaring enthusiasts wanting to get up into the blue.

In single-tow operations it takes about 15 minutes for a plane to tow a sailplane up to 2,000 feet and then return to the takeoff area, land, and taxi to position to hitch up another sailplane. This waiting time is not by any means dead time to the student or experienced soaring pilot, for there are usually enough chores about the area to keep all busy who want to work. Two people must help roll the sailplane pilot in his craft to the hitch location. Others help to clear a newly landed glider from the strip, park it, and perhaps on a windy day, stand by a sailplane ready to grab a wing should the wind get too blustery or endanger the sailplane.

For those not closely involved with the activities, there is still the constant thrill of watching sailplanes circling lazily

Typical weekend scene at the soaring site. In this case it's a get-together of members of the Blue Ridge Soaring Society, New Castle, Virginia.

upward in a thermal, or watching the approach of an incoming sailplane, catching briefly its personable whistle as it skims by overhead.

For those operations equipped with radio whereby ground personnel can listen in or talk to the pilots, it is worth one's while to listen to the patter of those in the air. They can be heard as they maneuver through the sky searching for thermals or updrafts, commenting interestingly to each other about their interpretations of meteorological conditions, giving position reports or comparing the performance of their sailplanes.

chapter **4**

Facts About the Sailplane

SAILPLANES FALL INTO three classes. One is the two-seat trainer. Another is the medium-performance single-seater. There are also a few two-place models manufactured that fall into this second class. A third is the high-performance, competition sailplane. Another category, the powered sailplane, is a sort of hybrid sailplane and light airplane combination. Engine power is used to get the sailplane airborne and into an area of lift whereupon the engine is shut down and retracted into the fuselage. The pilot then soars as with an ordinary sailplane. If he loses lift, or wants to go off to find another thermal, he has the option of elevating and using the engine.

The average sailplane weighs 400-500 pounds, but light weight and delicate appearance should mislead no one into thinking sailplanes are fragile. Moreover the high-performance models are aero-dynamically advanced and extraordinarily efficient aircraft. Sailplanes are built to withstand greater stresses than airplanes in the normal modes of flying, but they are not usually designed for aerobatics.

The wing of one of the sleekest reaches out 70 feet from tip to tip. Viewed from afar, these wings are so narrow that they look like streamlined pencils. The longer the wing and the narrower the chord (the width) of the wing, the more efficient the sailplane will be at low speeds.

For some years after gliding began, a few imagined the possibility of such a glider being sustained in the air purely by the air currents in the atmosphere. Once gliders got into the air, gravity took hold and inexorably pulled them towards the earth in gliding, gradually decending flight, a certain number of feet downward for a certain number of feet forward as gravity and the design of the particular glider dictated. Most early gliders came down one foot for about every eight feet of forward flight. The ratio of the number of feet the glider went forward to the number of feet it sank in the air became known as the glide ratio.

GLIDE RATIO

Glide ratio, also referred to as "lift-over-drag" is a frequently discussed term in soaring. It is perhaps the best characteristic from which to judge how a sailplane will perform.

The ratio is a comparison or ratio of the units of distance the sailplane flies forward in still air to the loss of altitude comparably measured over that distance. The two-place sailplanes have about 25:1 ratio, which means that in 25 feet of forward flight they descend one foot. Competition sailplanes have unbelievably high ratios of close to 50:1! Anything above 30:1, however, is considered high performance. Thus, a sailplane with a 30:1 glide ratio, when released one mile high, theoretically will glide 30 miles before touching ground even without using any thermal or other lift-giving force.

Another way of appreciating the glidability of a sailplane is to compare it with the old well-known Piper (Cub) J3C-65. This ultra-light, single-engine airplane has a 10:1 glide ratio. Thus, the glide ratio of the average sailplane betters that of the Cub and comparable light planes by about three to one.

SINK

Sink is a term used to indicate how fast a sailplane loses altitude in still air when descending at its rated glide ratio. When sink is given as two feet per second, for instance, it means a sailplane loses two feet of altitude per second while gliding in still air. This sink rate, of course, should give the pilot more than a 40-minute flight, if he was released at a one mile (5,280 feet) altitude (above ground, not sea level).

Another comparison between the performance of a sailplane and a small powered airplane will serve to underscore the importance of sink as well as to highlight again the average sailplane's exceptional rate of climb.

A sailplane off the tow is always descending, in relation to the body of air through which it is flying. Whether the aircraft is rising or falling in relation to the earth, however, depends on its sink rate compared with the direction (up or down) and speed of the surrounding air. High performance sailplanes have a minimum sink rate of less than 2 feet per second. Updrafts of air, in contrast, may easily reach a velocity of 1,000 feet per minute, or about 16.5 feet per second. Under these conditions, a sailplane would achieve a climb rate superior to that of many small powered aircraft.

THE WING IS THE THING

Good wing (also known as an airfoil) design makes prolonged soaring possible. Through the wing the sailplane gets its lift, or ability to rise into the air. A cross section of a wing is called an airfoil section; it is the basic unit of lift within the wing. The important thing is that the lifting ability of the wing is related to the shape of this section.

In order for an airfoil section to produce lift, it first must have forward motion. The faster the forward movement, the greater is the potential for increasing lift.

The air offers little resistance to a well-designed moving airfoil section. Since it is streamlined, it does not break up or disturb the air. However, if the airfoil is tipped upward at the front, or leading edge, as it is known, two separate lifting forces develop.

The bottom of the airfoil compresses the air underneath. This forms an invisible hill of air pressure that the airfoil rides up and runs over. Another way of explaining what occurs is to say that the compressed air pushes up against the bottom, forcing the wing upward.

A second force develops as the leading edge of the airfoil

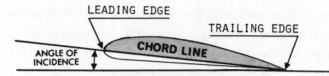

LINE PARALLEL TO LONGITUDINAL AXIS

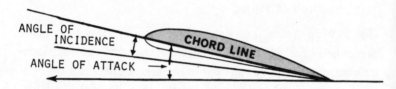

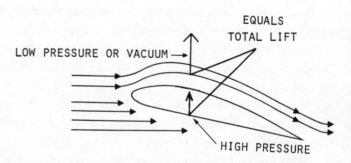

How lift develops.

gets higher than the trailing edge. When this happens, the air pressure above the surface of the airfoil falls off—it becomes less, or "thin." Since the airfoil is driving forward so fast that other air cannot rush in to fill the space and restore normal balance where the air is at low pressure or thin, a vacuum develops. The wing tends to be sucked into this vacuum and thus is identified the second lifting force.

Since the length of the wing is a countless number of airfoil sections, two forces pull and push upwards to lift the wing or create "lift." Thus, the sailplane gets its lift from forward speed, its airfoil shape and the angle in which the pilot places the wing during forward flight. This angle is called the "angle of attack."

It is well to mention at this point that if the wing's angle of attack is made too great, severe eddies form above and behind the wing. They decrease or destroy the vacuum, and if the vacuum decreases too much, the wing will not be able to produce enough lift, and what is known as a "stall" starts to develop. If this is allowed to happen, the sailplane will literally begin to fall until the pilot reduces the angle of attack enough so the sailplane can develop lift again. The pilot always tries to keep enough lift so as to never get dangerously close to a stall. But stalls and recoveries from stalls are practiced in lessons to acquaint a student with how they "feel." It is usually simple and easy to recover from a stall merely by putting the plane's nose down slightly until it recovers air speed.

GRAVITY

Well-designed aircraft glide or slide downward through the air when in free motorless flight, much like sleds slide down a snowy slope. Gravity is the force that draws them down. Placed in rising winds or thermals, motorless aircraft with good flight characteristics can defy gravity so long as the upward velocity of the air currents is greater than the sailplane's sink rate.

On every soaring flight a pilot will have to glide at times, since gliding is a part of any flight. The difference comes when the pilot gets lift from the forces in the sky. Then he soars.

INERTIA

Inertia is a bit more difficult to comprehend. It is also a powerful force. It is best described as the tendency of a sailplane, or other body, to remain at rest or to continue in flight in the direction in which it is already moving. It takes force to start to move a body that is at rest, and it takes force to stop the body that is already in motion.

IMPORTANCE OF AIR SPEED

The student soaring pilot should know what is meant by air speed and ground speed. It is customary for the nonflyer to think of speed in terms of how fast an automobile is going over the ground. In flying, the air speed of an aircraft is almost always different than ground speed. Its ground speed between two points may have been calculated at 100 miles per hour, whereas the air speed indicator may have read 150 miles per hour. In this case there must have been a head wind of 50 miles per hour so that although the plane had an air speed of 150 miles per hour it was making only 100 miles per hour over the ground.

The air speed indicator tells the pilot his speed through the air. In a sailplane the pilot also gets a feeling for air speed from the sound that the aircraft makes as it moves through the air and by sensing its pitch or attitude with respect to the horizon.

Typical sailplane cruising speed is 50 miles per hour. Thus, within limits, a pilot increases speed to gain better control of his aircraft. Too much speed, of course, is dangerous. All air speed indicators have a red dot or line on the dial to show the maximum safe limit. The aircraft must not be flown above this speed because this would create the possibility of structural damage.

STALL

Manufacturers establish and publish the stalling speed of their sailplanes. The pilot must keep the sailplane flying faster than this speed or the support of the wings becomes less than the weight of the sailplane, and the sailplane figuratively stops in the air momentarily, or stalls. Thus if the stall speed is 35 miles per hour, it is necessary to fly at more than that speed at all times to avoid stalling.

As a matter of fact, even though the specifications may give 35 miles per hour, the pilot will perhaps not go less than 40 miles per hour when carrying a maximum load and also when banking or turning. Under these conditions the sailplane is apt to stall at higher than the speed specified for that sailplane. The pilot merely adds a few extra miles per hour speed as a safety factor.

It is easy to recognize when a stall is imminent, and it is also easy to prevent one from occurring. It is just necessary to recognize the symptoms. The sound of wind dies away, the pressure on the controls decrease and they become what pilots call "mushy." When this starts happening, all the pilot has to do is to push forward on the stick to cause the nose to lower. Then the sailplane picks up speed and maneuvering control is regained. The important thing is to be constantly on the alert and not let the speed get too low, especially when at low altitude where a recovery dive of some hundreds of feet would be out of the question.

Many soaring students, nevertheless tend at first to maintain too steep a descent, presumably feeling it safer to do this than risk a stall. Most instructors will correct this, however, because too great a rate of descent is inefficient soaring and in conditions of good lift might waste a great deal of it. The right sensitive touch—enough to avoid stalling and at the same time the right sailplane attitude to capitalize on even a small amount of lift—is what soaring's all about. Learn the sailplane's stalling speed when flown as usually loaded. Thereafter keep an eye on the air speed indicator at intervals; it will quickly tell if the sailplane's attitude is inefficient—that is, nose too much down, excessive speed; nose too much up, speed falls off. Fortunately, one does not need to be too much preoccupied watching the instrument panel; maintaining the correct glide and attitude becomes a matter of recognizing the correct "feel" of the controls and eventually corrections, as necessary, are made subconsciously.

LOADING

A serious source of sailplane accidents, especially among inexperienced pilots, is improper aircraft loading. The same considerations which require the pilot to keep the gross weight and the center of gravity within the prescribed limits in a power plane apply to the sailplane. Most sailplanes have a loading chart in them, and pilots should be able to calculate quickly and accurately whether the load distribution is safe. The light weight of sailplanes relative to the passenger load, makes this a matter of utmost importance. In some of the lighter, more sensitive sailplanes, the passing of even a heavy camera from one seat to the other can make enough of a change in the center of gravity so that it is noticed by the pilot.

A tail-heavy sailplane will stall more easily and be more difficult to pull out of a spin. Also, too light a load may cause a problem. Some sailplanes are potentially uncontrollable with a single occupant under 125 pounds, and no ballast. Schools and clubs use bags of lead shot as ballast, and the young, light of weight—especially women students—should expect to ride with some ballast under the seat. Minimum as well as maximum loads should be posted in the aircraft, but the pilot is responsible for obtaining this information, wherever it is kept and following it.

Every pilot should understand the theory and techniques of solving problems affecting center of gravity, but for practical purposes he should also have access to the loading graph or *moment envelope* of every sailplane he uses. These will save him time on the field and reduce the opportunities for errors of calculation. If these are not provided by the manufacturer, an aircraft mechanic or engineer can devise them.

Incidentally, in calculating sailplane loads, it is necessary to count everything not a part of the original air-frame— not excepting parachutes and oxygen equipment. Do not use a hypothetical estimate of 170 pounds per passenger; get the exact weight.

If anyone has ever seen a seagull trying to get off the beach with an oversized clam in its beak, he can appreciate the importance of a few and poorly distributed excess pounds in the sailplane load. And, if a student wants to fly like a bird, he has to learn to think like one.

NOMENCLATURE

In no other form of recreation is it so necessary to know the "lingo" of the sport. Many words the novice will already know. Others will be entirely new since they apply only to soaring. Knowing them will not only mean safer soaring, but will also go a long way towards getting good communications between the student and the instructor. Some terms refer to sailplane parts such as aileron and empennage. Others to flying the sailplane such as lift, yaw and angle of attack. Skid has a special meaning to soaring that it has to no other aircraft or flying techniques. Thus, it is important to look over the Glossary at the end of the book and refer to it for the precise meaning of a new term.

PARTS OF THE SAILPLANE

With some minor exceptions, the parts of a sailplane are quite like any other aircraft without its engines. The fuselage is suspended from the wing midway between the wing sections. The pilot compartment is at the nose with instruments on a panel in the front. Most frequently, the tail assembly, or empennage consists of the vertical stablilizer (fin) with rudder attached and a horizontal stabilizer with

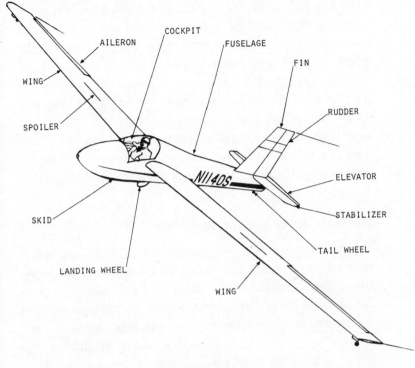

Parts of a sailplane.

elevators hinged to it. In some designs, however, there is no stabilizer, since the entire horizontal element moves as an elevator. In other designs these elements are not vertical and horizontal but form a "V" or "butterfly tail" shape.

The wing has ailerons to enable the pilot to make turns. The cockpit has pedals through which the feet control the rudder, and the usual stick for control of ailerons and elevator. How these operate to fly the sailplane are discussed in Chapter V.

Where the sailplane most departs in structure from an airplane other than having no engine is in its undercarriage.

This, more than likely, is a single central wheel, in some cases supplemented by a plywood, plastic or metal skid sweeping from the nose of the sailplane to just short of the wheel. This skid protects the nose and is also used for braking when the pilot noses the sailplane forward against the ground to use friction on the skid to bring the craft to a quick stop. A very few sailplanes have no wheel and land on skids only. Others have no external skid, but the base of the nose is reinforced to serve the same purpose as a skid. On most high-performance sailplanes the wheel is retractable.

PUTTING THE SAILPLANE TOGETHER

To those familiar with wooden gliders as used years ago, it may come as a distinct surprise to learn that sailplanes today can be dismantled. Occasionally sailplanes can be found made of rigid structures which cannot be taken apart for shipment in trailer-tow style, but these are now rare. Generally, manufacturers world-wide are producing sailplanes that can be readily dismantled and placed in trailers.

It is good to know something about taking a sailplane apart and putting it together, for it is certain that there will be many occasions when an owner will pull up to the air park with his trailered sailplane in tow behind his car. In these cases it will be possible to lend a hand. Or a pilot may need help in disassembling his craft. These are often team efforts, an owner looking for willing but experienced hands.

Assembling or disassembling a sailplane is probably one of the best ways to get to know how one is built and to get acquainted with its parts. Feeling the sturdiness of its parts and seeing the way they are joined together goes a long way towards instilling knowledge and confidence in this robust

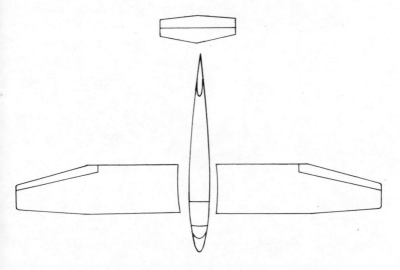

Sailplanes can readily be dismantled and transported in trailers.

craft. Furthermore, if one knows how to help in assembly and disassembly there is a good chance of being invited to help crew a cross-country flight. (Crewing is discussed in Chapter VIII.)

There is a systematic procedure for putting a sailplane together. This will be outlined under erection instructions in the sailplane's technical manual. Usually, the owner will direct the work. Though a sailplane is sturdy when fully assembled, some wrong move in handling wing section or stabilizer might easily damage it. There are right ways to pick up a wing, and some very wrong ones.

The most serious concern when putting a sailplane together is the prevailing wind velocity. If the wind is strong, it is best to work in a sheltered place. Sometimes this is not possible since many soaring sites are out in the

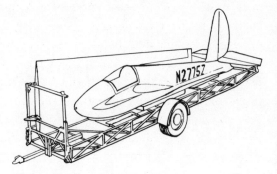

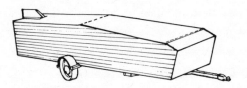

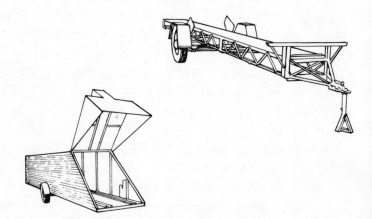

Typical sailplane trailer—most enclose the plane affording all-weather protection.
Some can be taken completely apart or optionally used compartment-fashion.

open quite far from the shelter of a hangar or woods. If wind cannot be avoided, it is best to turn the wings so that trailing edges face into the wind and are low.

Each wing section is best carried by two people—one person at each end. Parts should be lowered gingerly and rested on level ground or padded surfaces. Especially with the wings, use a sliding motion when putting them down to avoid puncturing or marring the skin with weed stubble or twigs.

Until the individual owns his own sailplane, it is a very good idea to confine his first contributions mostly to the brawn and leave the problem of placing and securing bolts and pins up to the owner.

Most owners have their own system for putting their sailplanes together—probably a bit different from the way prescribed in the manual, so it is a good idea to find what the owner wants done and then heed his instructions. They usually take one job at a time and finish it. They make certain that wing, main spar bolts, drag spar bolts, struts and tail surfaces are in place, bolted, if appropriate, or otherwise secured. Next, controls are connected and checked. This is followed by connecting the instruments and setting them. If the canopy must be installed, this is usually done last. There is a special place for tools. Small parts go in a box or in the cockpit map pocket—they are not put down in the grass or into someone's pocket where they can easily be lost!

Owners will make a thorough check to see that all tools are recovered, item for item, and then they search the cockpit to see that no tools or gear have been left there that should be properly stored in the automobile or trailer.

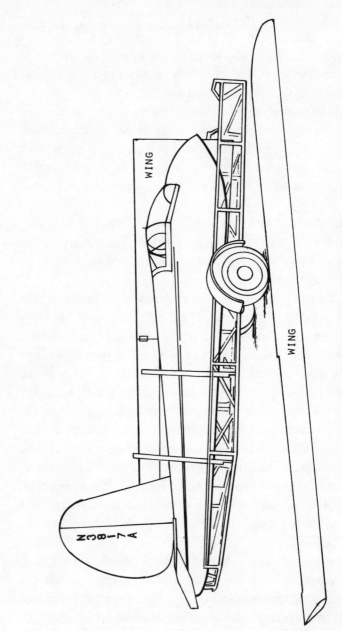

WING

WING

N38-17A

A sailplane partially loaded on its trailer.

chapter 5

Controlling the Sailplane

THE FUNDAMENTALS OF controlling the sailplane consist in knowing how to operate the ailerons, the elevator, the rudder, the spoilers and the wheel brake. Control of the sailplane is exerted through these parts from the cockpit by the pilot. He moves the control stick and rudder pedals in unison to turn left or right or to make climbing or diving turns. To climb or dive straight ahead, he uses stick alone. Spoilers, which may be raised or lowered on the wings, are used to cause the sailplane to lose altitude at a faster rate than normal.

THE CONTROLS

Control Stick

In most sailplanes the control stick is just as described, a broomstick-looking handle, which may or may not have a molded rubber grip, and which comes out of the floor and up between the knees of the pilot. He holds the top usually with one hand, the other remaining free to handle other controls.

Below the floor and out of view, the stick is pivoted. Control cables or rods attached to the bottom of the stick run to the ailerons and the elevator. The stick can be moved forward, backward, right, left, or in a circle.

Rudder Pedals

Two rudder pedals, one for each foot, are in front of the pilot and below the instrument panel. They are installed near the floor so that the pilot can comfortably place his feet on them. They are connected by cables to the rudder.

Ailerons

The two ailerons, one fitted into and hinged to the trailing edge of each wing, are movable panels that extend a third of the wing to its tip. Rods connect the ailerons to each other and to the stick in the cockpit.

Through the ailerons the pilot can stop the sailplane from rolling, that is, from tipping around its longitudinal axis, or he can bring the wings to a horizontal position or intentionally start a roll.

Suppose the pilot wants to bank the sailplane to the right.

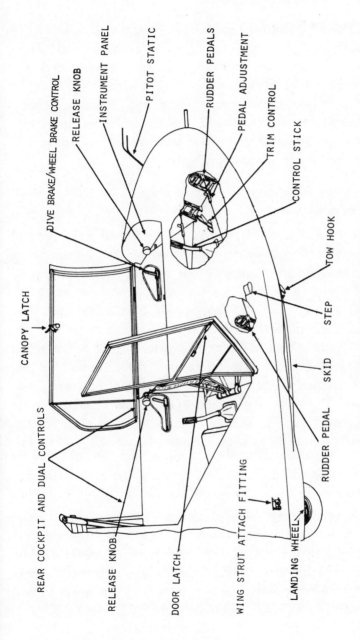

Features and controls of a two-place sailplane.

CANOPY LATCH

DIVE BRAKE/WHEEL BRAKE CONTROL

RELEASE KNOB

INSTRUMENT PANEL

PITOT STATIC

RUDDER PEDALS

PEDAL ADJUSTMENT

TRIM CONTROL

CONTROL STICK

TOW HOOK

STEP

SKID

RUDDER PEDAL

WING STRUT ATTACH FITTING

LANDING WHEEL

DOOR LATCH

RELEASE KNOB

REAR COCKPIT AND DUAL CONTROLS

To do so, he pushes the stick to the right. The right aileron thereupon goes up, which decreases lift in the right wing, hence it dips. Simultaneously, the left aileron goes down, increasing the lift of the left wing, causing this wing tip to rise. This combined action, when smoothly and properly coordinated with right rudder movement, results in a bank. It is important to realize that although both ailerons move at once, they move in opposite directions.

Elevators

The elevators are hinged to the horizontal stabilizer and together form a single airfoil. They give the pilot the means to change the sailplane's pitch attitude. When the stick is pushed forward, the elevators move down, increasing the lift in this airfoil combination, which forces the tail of the sailplane up and the nose down.

Elevators control the angle of attack of the wings. When the stick is pulled back, for example, the tail lowers, the forward edges of the wings raise, increasing the angle of attack. This vertical movement of the sailplane, induced by its elevators, is the motion called "pitch", which is the movement of the sailplane about its lateral axis.

Rudder

The rudder controls the movement of the sailplane about its vertical axis. This movement is called "yaw." The rudder is hinged to the vertical stabilizer, often called the fin. Its action is much like that of the elevators except that it swings in a different plane, going from side to side instead of up and down. Control cables lead to the rudder pedals.

The rudder does for the sailplane much as a rudder does for a boat. Pressing the left rudder pedal causes the trailing edge of the rudder to swing to the left and the nose to turn to the left. In a sailplane, however, a turn is based primarily on banking, with the rudder used only to overcome the customary yaw that occurs in the direction opposite the turn.

The articulation of the rudder-bar, rudder movement to produce a left turn may run counter to a novice's previous experience. Pushing the left handlebar of a bicycle or motorcycle turns the vehicle to the right, while pushing the left part of the rudder bar causes the sailplane to turn left. This can take some getting used to before flight, and may be mildly confusing during introductory flights. Still, it quickly becomes a natural thing to do since the rudder-bar movement coordinates with the stick, each requiring pressures to the right to make a bank to the right.

Spoilers

Some sailplanes have a spoiler installed on each wing midway between the forward and trailing edge on the upper surface which, when raised, causes the sailplane to lose altitude. They do just what the name implies, they spoil the air flow over the wing, thereby reducing lift and increasing drag.

Spoilers are most frequently used in the landing approach. The pilot pulls the handle in the cockpit that is connected by cables to the spoilers and obtains a high sink rate with no loss of speed. He can thus come over a high fence or telegraph cable and still land in a small field. If he sees he is going to be short at the landing touch-down point, he closes the spoilers a notch or so, thereby lessening drag, and increasing his glide distance. Then as he again decides he needs them, he raises them, and when the need occurs for fast braking during ground roll out he can apply full spoilers, which activates a mechanical brake in the landing wheel.

THE FEEL OF THE CONTROLS

The speed of a sailplane is reflected through the controls to the pilot. When moving through the air at high speed, as when diving, the air whipping by puts pressure on the ailerons, rudder and elevator surfaces in proportion to the speed. Because of this pressure it becomes harder to move the stick and the rudder pedals. They feel tighter than usual. At the same time, the faster the speed, the less control movement is necessary to get the sailplane to respond. But when a sailplane's speed is quite low, pressures on the external control surfaces drop, the stick and rudder pedals become loose, or "mushy," and it takes a great deal more movement of controls to get the sailplane to respond.

INSTRUMENTS FOR SAFE SOARING

Whereas participants in other sports use tools, bats, balls, tents, or other paraphernalia, in soaring the pilot uses instruments. These primarily consist of the air-speed indicator, the variometer and the altimeter.

Most sailplanes will carry five instruments. A high performance, competition sailplane, however, may carry seven or more. Actually, the use intended of a sailplane determines what instruments are installed. Trainers mainly need only a variometer, airspeed indicator, and altimeter.

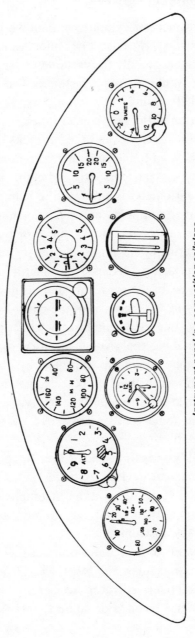

Instrument panel in a competition sailplane.

Soaring, by its very nature, cannot be exploited to its fullest possibility without the pilot using instruments. Without them, especially the variometer used to sense rising air, soaring would in many instances become little more than extended gliding. Few pilots are able to sense the gentle elevation of the sailplane as it begins to move upward in a thermal's upcurrent and the lift picks up. Without the variometer he might miss such thermals completely.

The altimeter and airspeed indicator are needed for safety. The variometer is employed to help gain attitude efficiently. But instruments alone do not make soaring enjoyable. It is one of the incongruities of flying a sailplane that most soaring pilots admit, but the joy of soaring comes when instruments are furthest from their minds.

The acute use of the eyes, ears and, as mentioned earlier, a sense of flying by "the seat of the pants" are vital to efficient soaring. In pre-soaring history, glider pilots measured climb by watching the ground fall away or by estimating how much they might be climbing by the degree their glider's nose was inclined . They also gauged speed by the whistle of air in the struts and the interval it took the glider to pass over some tree or crossroad—a very inaccurate system, indeed!

These bodily sensations have been long superceded by electro-mechanical devices as better indicators of motion and attitude. Because of the uncomplicated nature of primary training flights, however, some training sailplanes have few, if any, instruments.

As a sailplane pilot becomes more proficient and gets the yen to range, maneuver and test the clouds, he will want to add a turn and bank indicator, accelerometer, thermometer and an artificial hizon. For some flights the FAA makes radio mandatory. Also, there is general agreement that when soaring above 10,000 feet altitude, a pilot should don an oxygen mask.

Air Speed Indicator

This is the air equivalent of the automobile's speedometer, telling the speed the sailplane is moving through the air. It may be calibrated in miles, knots or kilometers per hour.

Altimeter

An altimeter tells how many feet the sailplane is above either sea level or a particular place on the earth for which it is set. It is a gauge that reads altitude by changes in pressure upon a diaphragm within the altimeter. As the sailplane rises into thinner air where pressure is less, the diaphragm reacts, causing the hand of the altimeter to show a higher altitude.

The altimeter must be adjusted for local barometric readings by turning a knob. The pilot learns the local barometric pressure by calling an airport weather service or someone in the control tower, usually the latter. He adjusts the altimeter to correspond with the local correct barometric reading before takeoff. Aloft, this gives him altitude above sea level. In most soaring flights, this is sufficient.

Altimeters give readings in feet and many are accurate to within plus or minus 10 feet of actual altitude. Some altimeters have three hands. One shows a 1,000-foot altitude increase by a complete 360 degree sweep of the hand. The second shows 10,000 feet, the third, 100,000 feet. Actually, however, 30,000 or 50,000 feet are the usual upper readings on altimeters.

Variometer

Sometimes referred to as a climb indicator, also as a vertical speed indicator, the variometer tells the pilot his rate of change of altitude.

As with the altimeter, this change takes place when the barometric pressure changes. It is the instrument most closely watched, for it is sensitive to the most subtle changes in lift, giving immediate clues to the presence of an unseen thermal or other lifting air force.

Although the basic principle upon which all variometers are designed is the change in barometric pressure, there are a number of distinctly different variometers manufactured.

One has a dial face similar to that of the altimeter with the hand moving into either a plus or minus area indicating the rate of climb in feet.

The most commonly used is the pellet variometer. It is highly sensitive and the favorite of soaring pilots. It also is relatively inexpensive and reliable. Its design shown in the accompanying illustration is simple. Its action is equally uncomplicated.

As the sailplane goes lower, the air pressure (atmospheric pressure) outside the sailplane gets greater and forces air into the outside opening of the variometer tube. This, in turn, causes the several red balls in the left tube to rise and the green ones to stay at the bottom or descend to the bottom and seal the tube at that point.

If the sailplane gains altitude, the pressure within the

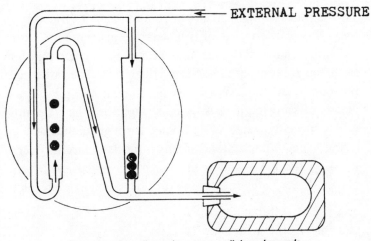

Operation of a pellet variometer as sailplane descends.

system, being greater than that outside, causes a reverse actions of the balls. The green ones go up in their tube. The
red go down to seal their tube.

By closely watching the instrument's action, the pilot can
tell when he is going up or when down and at what rates.
The higher the rate, the higher the balls will go up in the
tube, dropping gradually as the rate slows down. Beginning
pilots find the action of this clever instrument one of the
most absorbing phenomena on the instrument panel.

Compass

Except for cross-country flying and an occasional need to
get one's bearings while in a cloud or when leaving one, the
compass is rarely needed. However, it is found in most
instrument panels.

Bank and Turn Indicator

This is an essential instrument to assure pilot efficiency in blind flying. It consists of two separate instruments, a turn indicator and a ball-bank indicator. The former registers sailplane rotation around the vertical axis. The latter tells the lateral attitude. With this instrument the pilot has a means of knowing if he is flying straight or if he is turning; it is especially valuable in flying through clouds. Cloud flying in the United States in any aircraft is carefully regulated by the FAA and is infrequently carried out in sailplanes. Indeed, due to extreme turbulence, hail, icing condi-

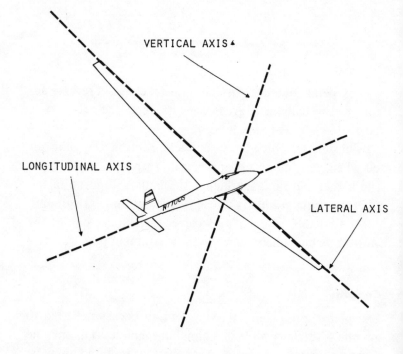

VERTICAL AXIS

LONGITUDINAL AXIS

LATERAL AXIS

Axes of the Sailplane.

tions and lightning, cloud flying in sailplanes can be an unpleasant and dangerous experience.

Radios

It is estimated that not more than one quarter of the sailplanes in use in the U.S. are equipped with radios. Thus, it will be a rare occasion where a student will have the opportunity to use a sailplane having a radio.

The newcomer to soaring will most likely have most of his experience with radios when he engages in cross-country crewing. He may have to man the portable shortwave radio carried in the car with the empty sailplane trailer hitched behind, chasing the pilot across country. These radios may range from a small "handy talkie" to an advanced, longer range and heavier model. All models, however, are fairly easy to operate.

There are two essentials to their operation. The first concerns care and maintenance. Both sets must be operating, the frequencies and dial setting must be carefully understood before the start of a mission, and both sets should be tested with the users actually in the respective car and sailplane in which the sets will be used. It is surprising how frequently a radio can develop problems when mounted in a particular car, a happenstance stemming perhaps from the peculiarities of the metal in the car body, the car's electrical system and its engine operation.

The other essential is that if the radio is battery operated, and if it is uncertain whether the battery is strong, a spare battery should be carried.

Some clubs have their operations control centers equipped with radio, many of their members having sailplanes equipped with radios. These clubs are the exception, however, since by far the majority of clubs and small commercial soaring facilities simply do not use radios. For the most part, there is little need for expensive radio equipment in soaring.

Many pilots like to maintain a two-way radio hookup to the rest of the family, hence they keep one of the sets in the family car back at the field. Radios used this way have done much to put the grounded members into the sport, and they lessen the chance of boredom to those waiting the return of the sailplane.

There is reason to believe there will be a growing use of radios in the sport. Carrying a radio enables the sailplane to fly in the highly regulated, high density traffic areas where all aircraft entering are required to use radios. Then, too, radios will enable soaring pilots to range farther, entering areas now largely restricted to non radio-equipped aircraft.

chapter 6

Flying the Sailplane

WITH BUT FEW exceptions, sailplanes do not have their own power. They must depend on some outside source to get into the air. In the early decades of the century, five to ten men grabbed a tow rope hitched to the nose of a glider and ran as fast as possible down hill against the wind, hoping to get the glider going fast enough so that it could get airborne. Frequently they failed, completely winded from the exertion.

Galloping horses also towed gliders into the air. Later, a jacked-up rear auto wheel, converted to a make-shift winch, "winched" gliders into the air, after which the pilots released from the winch line to get what lift they could. Glider pioneers also used the automobile, which sped over the turf, glider in tow, much the way kite flyers run with a kite. Some daredevils even took off from the edge of a precipitous cliff, others tried being carried to three or four thousand feet in a glider hitched to a balloon and then released.

Today, the three commonly-used launch systems are the winch launch, the auto-tow and the aerotow, with the aerotow being by far the most popular in the United States. Winch launching, however, is still favored in England and Germany.

LAUNCHING METHODS

Winch Launch

This is done by attaching the sailplane nose's center-of-gravity hitch to a long steel cable connected to a motor-driven winch located several thousand feet away. On signal, the winch operator reels in the cable at about 50 miles per hour. For the first hundred feet of altitude the sailplane rises slowly but then begins to ascend at about a 40 degree angle. When it reaches about 1,000 feet of altitude, it is usually almost directly over the winch; and by this time the pilot has released.

Auto Tow

This system is the least used in the United States of the three. However, it is the cheapest method, has the most readily available apparatus and launches the sailplane al-

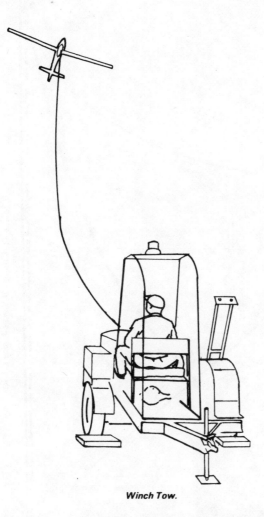

Winch Tow.

most as high as the better winches. With this system, the sailplane is simply attached by a long, thin steel cable to the back of an automobile. The car then pulls the sailplane until it gets to a height of about 1,300 feet, whereupon the pilot releases.

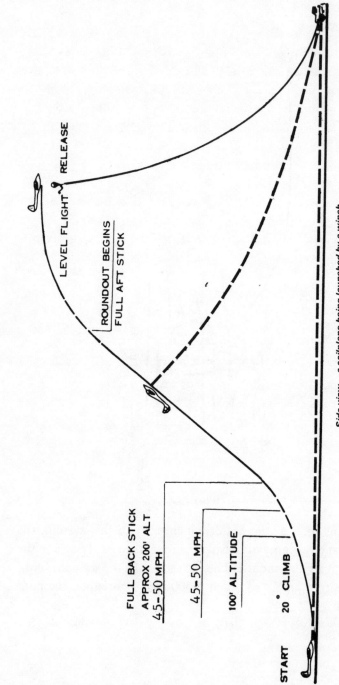

FULL BACK STICK
APPROX 200' ALT
45-50 MPH

45-50 MPH

100' ALTITUDE

20° CLIMB

START

LEVEL FLIGHT

RELEASE

ROUNDOUT BEGINS

FULL AFT STICK

Side view—a sailplane being launched by a winch.

Aerotow

With the aerotow, the sailplane nose hitch is attached by a polypropylene rope to a hitch in the tail of a single-engine light airplane. The airplane tows the sailplane to altitudes where suitable soaring conditions are believed to prevail. There the sailplane pilot releases from the tow aircraft.

Of the three methods, the aerotow gives the sailplane pilot the best chance of having a reasonably long flight, not only because he will get to a higher release altitude, but also because the tow pilot can take him to where the lift is. Winch launching, on the other hand, is the quickest way to get a sailplane into the air and is the system that gives sailplane pilots a lot of practice in takeoffs and landings.

GETTING THE FEEL OF THINGS

Flying is not natural to man. Walking is. Flying takes skill, and this skill must be acquired through study, instruction and actual flying. It is helpful to a prospective student to have confidence in the sailplane and the medium that gives the sailplane support and maneuverability. It is also important to know the sailplane and to get the "feel" of things. Some of the feel comes from doing the right things on the ground before flying.

Thus, it is a good idea before taking even an introductory flight to see if it is possible to arrange to climb into the cockpit of a sailplane while it is parked and do some mental browsing, combined, perhaps, with a bit of imaginative dreaming, manipulating the controls to bank to the right, climb as in a thermal or simulate a takeoff.

Cockpit Orientation

After settling down in the cockpit, study the surroundings. Inspect the instrument panel. It is a compact version of an automobile dashboard, and except for gas gauges and engine instruments, is almost identical with that of many light airplanes. In the automobile, the speedometer, gasoline gauge and other instruments are spread out. The sailplane instrument panel is narrow, fitting snugly into the limited space above the pilot's knees.

Get an idea of just where each instrument is and what it does. The variometer, indicating the rate at which the sailplane climbs or descends, is the instrument a sailplane pilot uses most because it is the one that senses the presence of a thermal, or lifting force. Become familiar with it.

Push the rudder pedals. Look back at the rudder and see that it moves to the right as the right pedal is pushed forward. Try to see how far it moves with different pressures.

Manipulate the stick. Notice that when pushed to the right the aileron of the right wing goes up and that of the left goes down. In flight this causes the sailplane to bank to the right. Now push the stick forward, which would make the nose go down and cause an increase of speed, and then move it back, which would make it go up and cause a decrease in speed. A sailplane pilot always works these controls before the flight, testing them to see if they move freely during his pre-flight check, and watching the control surfaces of the sailplane to see that they respond accordingly. This is, in fact, part of the pre-takeoff procedure in all aircraft.

Pull back on the air brake control. It is at the side of the cockpit. Notice how the panels raise from the top of the wing. These make the sailplane slow down in the air by creating turbulence in the stream of air passing over the wings which, in turn, reduces lift and speed, slowing the sailplane and causing it to lose altitude.

The Importance of the Safety Belt

Clamp into the safety harness and adjust the straps so that they bind slightly. The safety belt not only gives the pilot safety and a feeling of security, but it also is important in giving him a feeling of solidity and oneness with the sailplane. This tends to improve kinesthesis while in flight.

KINESTHESIS

It is highly important to relax while piloting, for when relaxed and only when relaxed, does the kinesthethetic sense operate properly. Soarers mention this word frequently, for in few other of mankind's activities does it play so important a part.

Kinesthesis (body sensations) is the feeling that comes to one from nerve endings located in muscles, tendons and joints. It is one of the senses, and, combined with vision, provides one of the reliable indicators to the mind of what is going on about the body. It combines with vision in flight, relying on the position of the horizon, when it can be seen, and on what the eyes see from the instruments when no horizon can be seen.

Rather than be sophisticated, it may be that a pilot will say, "I flew that one by the seat of my pants." What he really meant was that he relied upon kinesthesis. Perhaps he was entirely unfamiliar with the word, but he used the best way he could think of to express the operation of this very important human sense.

Bodily Responses

Many of a person's natural bodily responses to events in day to day living work to advantage in flight. It is well to know what some of these are and use them.

Recall that when a person turns his head to the right he is likely to incline it slightly. To bank a sailplane to the right (a maneuver which causes the right wing tip to dip as the sailplane pivots about it), the stick is moved to the right in a movement generally synchronized with the turning of the head and eyes in that direction.

Similarly, to look up, the head is tilted upward, a movement a pilot makes normally before climbing higher. It is just natural to synchronize pulling the stick towards the stomach as the head raises to look upward. Similarly for the movements of the other controls with one important exception.

It has become natural for men to expect to make a right turn while steering an automobile by turning the wheel to the right, using the hands to make the wheel turn. As far as the sailplane is concerned, to turn it to the right the pilot must make a foot movement that works against this experience. If he wishes to turn to the right, he presses his right foot against the rudder bar pushing it forward. Seemingly an unnatural move at first, it quickly becomes natural, especially when coordinated with the stick. By pushing the stick to the right, the right wing dips downward, and the combination of movements by the right foot and the hands in this way puts the sailplane into a banked turn.

FLYING THE SAILPLANE

Assume that it is the third instructional flight. It is 2:20 in the afternoon of a bright, slightly windy day and a few minutes before takeoff. Eight sailplanes are parked along the side of the field. An assortment of onlookers, school staff, private owners and an operations vehicle create a bustle of activity.

There is little time to waste. The tow plane is due to land in a few minutes, hitch up to the SGS 2-33 and takeoff with the sailplane in the next tow.

The Preliminaries

The instructor has already walked to the right wing. At the left wing a crewman has pushed the bag of lead shot to the ground, the bag that was lying on the wing as a weight to keep the wing from being lifted by the wind while it was parked.

The student gets to the tail right away, cups a hand under the horizontal stabilizer close to the fuselage, and raises the

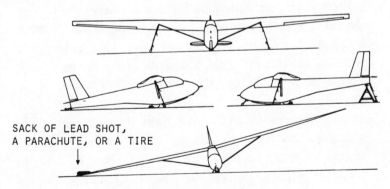

SACK OF LEAD SHOT,
A PARACHUTE, OR A TIRE

Protecting the sailplane from high winds.

tail. He follows the instructor's directions and helps push the sailplane the 20 or so yards to the takeoff point. Then he swings the tail to point the nose of the sailplane into the wind, which is coming directly down the runway. Whoever the student is, this is what he'd do next.

Watch the instructor, and follow him as he circles the craft, making his pre-flight check. He may appear somewhat casual. That is undoubtedly because he made an exhaustive preflight check early in the morning before the first student's flight.

Help raise the canopy. Push down on the nose of the glider and climb into the front seat. Shift around until the seat feels thoroughly comfortable, don the seat harness, clamping it securely. Make sure the shoulder strap is not too snug. Leave enough slack so there will be no problem in reaching to the release knob or the instrument panel.

Since the instructor has not yet climbed into the seat behind, work the controls to make a pre-flight check. The sailplane rocks a little as the instructor takes his seat, and it is possible to feel him nudge the pedals as he positions his feet on them.

There is so much going on there is scarcely time to look around to find the tow plane, whose engine is now audible. It appears taxiing up from the left front. Then suddenly all becomes quiet again as the instructor closes the canopy. It almost seems as though the tow plane has turned off its engine!

Sense the pressure on the stick right, then left, then on the pedals as the instructor checks the controls. When the ground crewman, holding the tow rope, hitches it to the nose, be prepared to test the release by pulling the red release knob on the instructor's orders. This is a customary

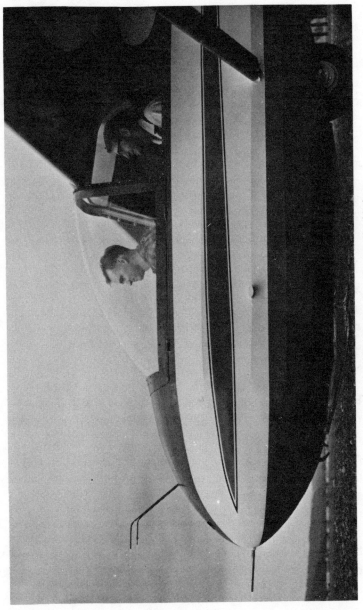

Student and instructor all set for tow line hitch-up.

check before each takeoff. The crewman stands to the front pulling the rope.

There is a tap on the shoulder and a "Pull the release!" from the instructor. Grab the knob. Good! There is a metallic ping as the rope releases. That checkout step is completed!

The crewman holding the rope lifts it in front of the canopy. This allows the pilot a close look at the rope. It looks new and staunch. The pilot has a right to reject the tow rope at this point, if he wishes to. The instructor makes a circle of his thumb and index finger, however, meaning okay.

The Takeoff

Since this is a one-man operation, the ground crewman, after attaching the tow rope to the sailplane, raises the slack rope overhead in signal to the tow pilot to move forward slowly to take up the slack. When the rope is taut, the crewman moves to the sailplane's wing tip. He checks the sky and the traffic pattern to be sure it is clear. When it is, he signals the instructor, "pattern clear." The instructor now signals to the crewman, "wing up." When the wing is raised, the instructor signals the tow plane by swinging the rudder from side to side. The tow plane pilot acknowledges this signal by fanning the tow plane's rudder.

Motor noise again becomes audible as the tow pilot powers up and starts forward, and now it happens! The nose of the sailplane is pulled upward by the rope attached to the belly, and the sailplane starts to move. The crewman runs for a few steps, holding the wing level. There is a drumming as the wheel trundles over the bumpy ground and an occa-

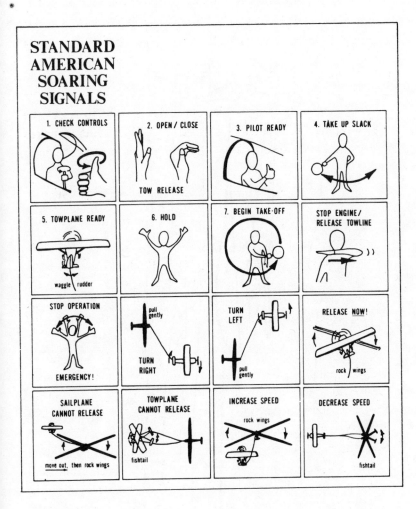

STANDARD AMERICAN SOARING SIGNALS

1. CHECK CONTROLS

2. OPEN / CLOSE
TOW RELEASE

3. PILOT READY

4. TAKE UP SLACK

5. TOWPLANE READY
waggle rudder

6. HOLD

7. BEGIN TAKE-OFF

STOP ENGINE / RELEASE TOWLINE

STOP OPERATION
EMERGENCY!

TURN RIGHT
pull gently
TURN LEFT
pull gently

RELEASE NOW!
rock wings

SAILPLANE CANNOT RELEASE
move out, then rock wings

TOWPLANE CANNOT RELEASE
fishtail

INCREASE SPEED
rock wings

DECREASE SPEED
fishtail

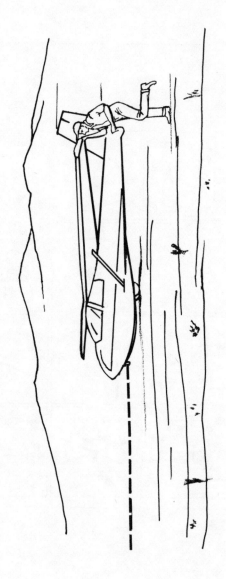

Running a wing.

sional slapping of weeds against the fuselage underbelly. The ground races towards and beneath the sailplane and within a few seconds—silence. The sailplane is in the air! The tow plane, some 150 feet ahead, is still rolling along the ground tugging valiantly. Then it, too, is in the air.

There is a bit of jostling at first, a shifting to left and then to the right, as the instructor must use large movements of the controls at these low speeds. He keeps the sailplane low and to the left of the tow plane to avoid the turbulent air in its wake and also to minimize the tow plane's task of climbing—gaining altitude. Feet and hands sense the various moves the instructor makes to keep the sailplane in position. The ground has receded below, there is an almost cloudless sky above. Shortly the tow plane pilot banks slowly to the left and starts on the long climb to the release altitude. Throughout the tow, the sailplane stays slightly above the airplane whose motor is now barely audible.

Free Flight

The tow rope sags a little, and then tightens again as the combination of sailplane and towplane pass through bumpy air. Notice that the airspeed indicator is reading about 65 miles per hour and that the altimeter has already swung by the first thousand foot mark and is moving steadily around the hundred foot mark. Within a few minutes 2,100 feet show on the altimeter—time for release

Just then the instructor says, "Release." Take a good hold on the red knob and pull. This time there is a sharp metallic ping, much stronger and louder than during the test on the ground before takeoff, and now the sailplane is flying alone!

There is almost an eerie silence, the jostling from the tow rope is gone. Immediately after release the instructor starts a bank to the right. The tow plane, in accordance with standard procedure, has banked off to the left and is already descending. The sailplane's air speed dips to 45 miles per hour during this turn, and as the pilot completes it he says, "Trim it slightly."

Reach for the lever between the knees and near the floor. This is the "nose trim." Pull the lever back several notches. "Two more," he says." Now the sailplane is in level flight, stable and seemingly ready to fly itself.

"Take the controls," the instructor then says.

As a student be prepared for this moment, since a student should have his feet and hands already on the controls and should have lightly followed the instructor's movements during the turn. The best thing to do is to get the sailplane flying level—a normal attitude which the instructor expects so that things are under control before the next maneuver. The sailplane comes out of its banked turn to the right and the wings now are level. The instructor is silent. Apparently he approves. Try holding the sailplane in this attitude for a few minutes. Isn't the feeling great!

Relax. The grip should be light, but firm enough to feel what is happening to the sailplane through the messages the controls send to the hand from the ailerons and elevator. It is not necessary to use a great amount of force to move the controls. Already a better sense of feel of what is going on through the controls can be noticed. This is to be expected, for no one is born with a polished pilot's coordination of eyes, balance and muscular control. It comes with practice. The instructor helps to correct errors as they occur, and coordination improves with each correction until it becomes second nature.

The instructor breaks the serenity. "Some left yaw," he requests.

Press the left rudder pedal. Notice how the nose turns to the left dutifully.

"Now right," comes the instructor's voice.

Press the right pedal, and the sailplane starts skidding to the right. In front on the outside of the canopy is a yellow, two-inch long yaw string, which is found on all sailplanes and is used as a yaw indicator. It streams to the right as the sailplane yaws to the right. Even with only the third lesson these maneuvers are getting to be routine, but the instructor is doing them so that they get to be second nature.

"Try a little left stick and left rudder," he says.

Since this is only the third instructional flight, do so rather gingerly. The effort works out fine. The left wing tip drops, the nose turns smoothly, and the sailplane makes a magnificent bank to the left.

This is all great fun, but a glance at the altimeter shows that this has cost 600 feet in altitude so far, since it now reads 1,500 feet. Leveling out again, the sailplane is in straight flight when there is a slight surging of the sailplane upward.

"Let me take over," comes from the instructor. That was the indication of a thermal, and he wants to try to stay in it. At this moment notice that the little red ball in the vario-meter has dropped to the bottom of the glass tube, while the green ball has jumped up midway. Now quickly the green ball drops and the red ball jumps up, and the sailplane is out of the thermal. The sailplane was going too fast, and the thermal area was too small to stay in it long.

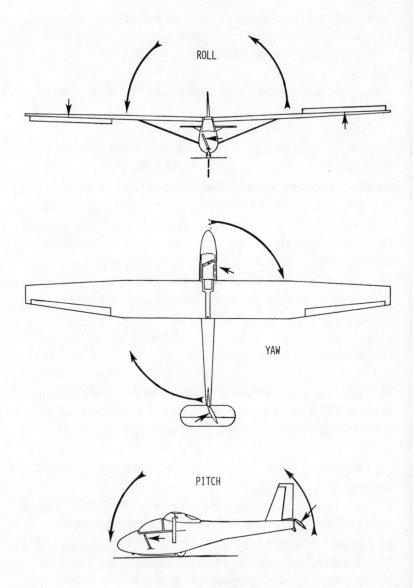

ROLL

YAW

PITCH

Now the sailplane is almost standing on the right wingtip as the instructor makes a 180 degree turn to go back and try to find the thermal. "Watch the variometer this time," says the instructor.

Sure enough, there is the same surge upward, the telltale indicator of a thermal. He has found it again!

"Take the controls," he says.

(The technique generally is to watch the variometer and try to feel which wing is being buoyed up by the lift. If the left wing presses up, turn left, into the lift. If the nose begins to rise, turn either left or right.)

Start a gentle bank to the right. Feel the lifting sensation. The instructor perceives there is not enough attention to the instruments. There is a nudge at the shoulder, and he says, "look at the second variometer." (One that has a scale and an indicator hand.)

Its hand is at 450 feet—meaning that the thermal is lifting the sailplane at 450 feet a minute, a pretty strong thermal.

"Try to stay with it awhile," he says.

Take firm control. It feels good, like a fast elevator. Suddenly there is a change in the feeling, as if the elevator has stopped rapidly for a floor. The green ball drops down in the tube. That is the end of the thermal.

The instructor says, "Look out to the right." He has spotted a large bird some distance away, its wings spread out in soaring flight. "Let's join him," he says.

It is a hawk, its wings motionless, soaring at the same height as the sailplane. His presence is usually a good indication of a thermal.

Push the stick to the left and forward ever so little and press the left pedal. Get enough of a turn to line up on the hawk, and then fly in level flight straight towards him. The instructor says nothing. Presumably all maneuvers are O.K.

The sailplane gets to within a few hundred feet of the hawk and seems to pass over a burble of air, but the vario-meter indicates that the lift is not strong enough to support the weight of the sailplane. The needle of the dial-type variometer hovers in the negative area.

The instructor says, "I guess it was strong enough for a hawk but not enough for us. I'll take over now," and there is the reassuring feel of his hands at the controls, a steadying assistance, a jiggling of the stick; and he is flying the sailplane. The altimeter reads 2,500 feet, so although the sailplane did not pick up altitude where the hawk was flying, it did in the previous area of lift. Indeed, the sail-plane had gained 400 feet since release. Not bad!

It is time to start back to the field.

Landing

Landing calls for more skill than new students acquire, so don't expect the pilot to turn over the controls again on this flight. Just pay attention now to what he is doing, the at-titude of the sailplane during the approach and the flareout and the braking procedures. Keep feet and hands at the con-trols, but do not interfere with their operation by the instructor.

Notice how the instructor is glancing in every direction. He is making sure that no other aircraft is in the vicinity. He also takes a look at the wind sock on the field to de-termine the direction of the wind. It has not changed since takeoff, so he plans to land in the same direction as the takeoff.

Since the sailplane is rather high and the entry point for the landing pattern is not too far away, he pulls the lever,

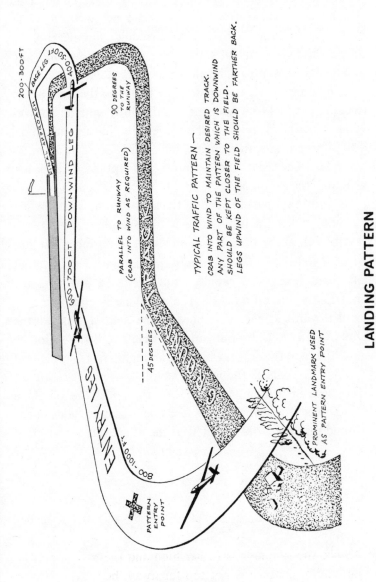

200-300FT

FINAL APPROACH

BASE LEG

400-500FT

DOWNWIND LEG

90 DEGREES TO THE RUNWAY

600-700 FT

PARALLEL TO RUNWAY
(CRAB INTO WIND AS REQUIRED)

45 DEGREES

ENTRY LEG

800-1000 FT

PATTERN ENTRY POINT

PROMINENT LANDMARK USED AS PATTERN ENTRY POINT

TYPICAL TRAFFIC PATTERN —

CRAB INTO WIND TO MAINTAIN DESIRED TRACK.
ANY PART OF THE PATTERN WHICH IS DOWNWIND
SHOULD BE KEPT CLOSER TO THE FIELD.
LEGS UPWIND OF THE FIELD SHOULD BE FARTHER BACK.

LANDING PATTERN

which raises the spoilers in the wings to get a rapid descent. Just short of the entry point, marked below by a white frame farm house with a red barn and silo nearby, he retracts the spoilers and starts the right turn that will take him into the entry leg. The altimeter reads 1,200 feet.

As he approaches the airstrip, he banks to the right again to come parallel to it and start on the downwind leg (downwind, since he is flying in the same direction as the wind). The airspeed indicator, meanwhile, is hovering at 55 miles per hour. The field is close now, and upturned faces are watching the sailplane.

He continues past the end of the strip and now at 400 feet altitude, makes the first left turn in the landing approach, a real breathtaking one. He is now on the base leg. He has barely leveled out when he puts the sailplane into another left turn, levels out rapidly, and lo, there ahead is the airstrip coming up quickly. The sailplane is gliding downward towards a fence that borders the field, a point all the pilots use as a "flare-out" marker. He keeps the sailplane nose aimed at the fence, which is coming up fast.

When it seems as though the sailplane is about to hit the fence, the instructor pulls back on the stick, the sailplane skims over it and flies a few feet above and parallel to the ground for about 200 feet. This is the "flare out." The speed

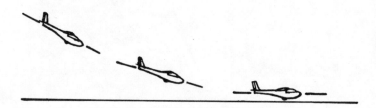

Landing flareout.

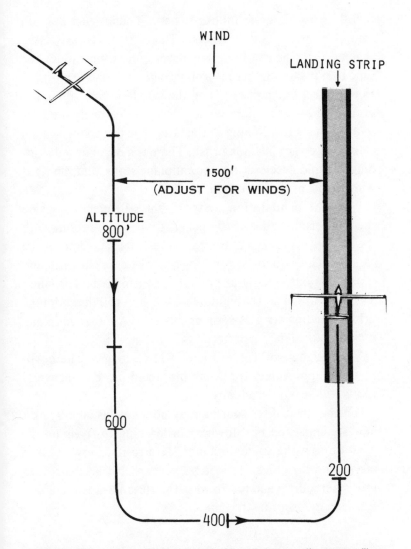

WIND

LANDING STRIP

1500'
(ADJUST FOR WINDS)

ALTITUDE
800'

600

200

400

Typical landing pattern—note that in both this and the preceding pattern illustration the turn from base leg to final is to the left or counterclockwise, the downwind leg being flown with the runway on the left. Suppose the wind direction was the opposite? Check this with an instructor. The same pattern might apply although it might be flown over terrain on the opposite side of the runway. There are sometimes pattern variations at various airports due to local conditions.

is still high—about 48 miles per hour. The instructor again smoothly opens the spoilers. There is that instinctive bracing for a hearty bump. It never comes, but about the time that it should, there is a slight bumping and drumming as the wheel touches, and then the sailplane rolls along the ground. Feel the stick move forward decisively and simultaneously the dipping of the nose. The instructor has decided to stop the headlong rush. There is a pronounced skidding, a rapid deceleration, the sailplane stops, and the right wing tip drops to the ground.

With the exhilaration of the flight still pent up inside there is certain to be a little nervousness and fumbling with the canopy release in assisting the pilot to remove the canopy. This is natural for a tyro until he has flown many times. Get out quickly as possible and run to the left wing. The pilot will be at the right one. Help him roll the sailplane off the landing strip as soon as possible. Another sailplane may be in the landing pattern.

More flights will follow. They will be longer. There will be more opportunity for doing more and more maneuvers. Skills will be built gradually.

Getting the feel for soaring may not come as quickly as a new student expects. Slowness in learning to fly is no indication that the student cannot learn to fly. Slow starters often outstrip quicker learners, perhaps because they are more methodical and retain what they learn, while the quick learner forgets his instruction.

chapter 7

Using Winds and
Clouds

SOARING COMBINES THREE things: pilot, sailplane, and the
atmosphere. The pilot provides the intellect, the sailplane
the means to fly, and the atmosphere provides the lift.

An understanding of the behavior of the atmosphere, or
meteorology, as it is known, therefore, goes hand in hand
with an understanding of soaring. In fact, it is not possible
to discuss soaring intelligently, or to become truly skilled in
the sport without a knowledge of at least some fundamentals of the behavior of the winds, thermals and clouds.

Some areas naturally provide many thermals and are
well-known to soaring pilots who converge on these areas

for hours of reliable pleasure. Some upward currents of air reveal themselves to the practiced eye, or through the actions of birds. Others must be hunted. It is these last, which in their discovery and capture, provide soaring's greatest thrills.

Upcurrents of sufficient strength can give a higher lift rate than the normal sink rate of a given sailplane. When a sailplane enters suitably strong upcurrents, it soars. Thus, the soaring pilot must find the upcurrents that are strong enough to enable him to soar.

Soaring students just starting out will get the basics of meteorology from their instructors and from materials provided by their schools. The discussion here is merely a brief consideration of meteorological phenomena, an introduction to a topic which in itself is a most fascinating and challenging subject. Countless hours of study could be devoted to it. Many pilots do just that.

As a beginning, however, consider the soaring pilot's hunt for a ridge lift, a sea breeze front, a wave, a thermal, or a likely-looking, lift-producing cloud, a search which starts immediately following release from the tow plane.

WIND

Every soaring pilot is concerned with wind before, during a part of, or in nearly all of each flight, and especially during landing, when wind strength and direction must be critically assessed. The tow plane always takes off towing the sailplane into the wind. With a stronger wind, the tow plane will takeoff in a shorter distance. Most pilots always want to know where the wind is coming from, as well as its speed.

There is also such a thing as too strong a wind for flying, particularly with light aircraft, as most tow planes are.

Winds encountered at ground level, on the whole, are the result of cool air masses that may either move leisurely or rush in swiftly to fill a low-pressure area. Although the phrase "low-pressure area" is frequently used by the weather man, it is doubtful if many understand its meaning, and fewer yet how it develops winds and what the factors are that influence the direction these winds will take.

As a simple approach, when the sun heats the earth, the earth, in turn, heats the air directly in contact with it. This warm air rises, forming into a thermal, and the surrounding cooler air moves in along the ground to replace the more buoyant warm air. This movement is commonly identified as wind. The layer of air feeding the thermal and felt as a breeze is irregular in thickness, but one never knows—it may be from several feet to several hundred feet thick.

Winds are also caused by forces other than the movement of air masses from a high- towards a low-pressure area, but not all these forces can be discussed.

SLOPE WINDS (RIDGE LIFT) (HILL LIFT)

A great air mass on the move and recognized as a wind, upon encountering a vertical obstacle, such as a wall or hill, sweeps up and over the obstacle. In doing so, it creates an effective, but invisible, wave formation in the air above the obstacle.

This produces an ideal soaring condition. The pilot flies the sailplane to the side where the wind hits the hill and rides the upsweeping air quite a respectable distance above the hill and at approximately 90 degrees to the direction of the wind. He rides the hill's length, or as far as he can or wishes to, taking advantage of that particular slope wind. Then, he turns outward from the hill and reverses his track. This is a procedure he can repeat as long as he is able to stay awake, and as long as visibility allows safe soaring, although with the approach of darkness the slope wind may diminish or die out entirely.

The actual pattern of the *hill lift* with relation to the hillside and top, and the height to which it rises varies with the velocity of the wind as well as the grade of the hillside. Under some circumstances, there is a "roll" pattern of turbulent air up against the hill. In general, the more abrupt or irregular the hillside, the more unpredictable the local turbulence, and the wider a berth it should be given, in the interest of safety. A gradually rounded hilltop will produce a gradually dimishing windward updraft, whereas a sheer cliff or an irregular promontory may produce freakish wind shifts or drops. The sailplane pilot has his faithful variometer to help him feel the thrust of the wind, but he must also depend on his eyes and the feel of the controls to judge and anticipate its behavior. He learns how to approach the windward side of the ridge with caution—at an angle that permits a quick, short turn away from the slope in case the expected lift is absent. Also he learns to use airspeed to traverse quickly through areas of zero or negative lift.

Certain hills in regions where there are steady, dependable winds have become known as sources of slope winds. Soaring pilots regularly congregate above them.

THERMALS

Thermals are choice lift producers for soaring fans, and the most sought after of the atmospheric phenomena, except

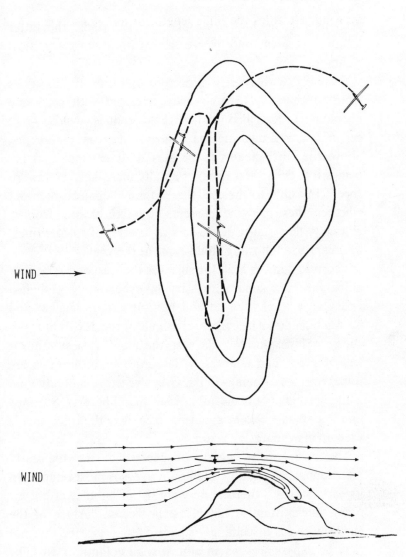

WIND ⟶

WIND

How a sailplane uses slope winds for lift in soaring.

perhaps for the high-atmosphere wave winds, the latter usually prevalent only where the location's topography is right.

Basically, a thermal is a current of warm air that rises from the earth. Thermals are associated with the same phenomena described earlier that produce winds. Over certain warm areas, such as large paved areas, the air just above the earth begins to be heated. It expands and becomes less dense and rises, gradually increasing in upward speed. Invisible to the eye, there is much conjecture about whether these upward currents are like smoke from a chimney, like a dust devil, or like a series of smoke rings. Frequently, a billowing cloud caps the thermal.

Thermal hunters look for surfaces that respond relatively quickly to the sun's rays—dry lake beds, dry ploughed fields, race tracks, paved and built-up areas, beaches and barren hillsides. The earliest thermals of the day usually occur over slopes that face the east (the angle of the sun thus is less oblique), and conversely, late-in-the-day thermals are found over west-facing slopes. Green vegetation of any kind is likely to invite downdrafts rather than updrafts. Swamps and wet areas are to be avoided, since there the solar heat is used up in evaporating water.

Thermals are strongest, of course, during the early afternoon when heating by the sun's rays is most intense. In its early stages a thermal may consist of bubbles of hot air rising intermittently. Later, as the heated surface of the earth produces a seemingly steady flow of air, the thermal may be experienced as an almost solid column of air. The thermal has no specific shape, of course, or area; it could be a hundred feet or less in diameter or it might be several hundred feet. Its form and area are determined by the

Soaring in a thermal.

"griddle" below and the movement of wind. Indeed, winds of more than 20 mph tend to break up thermals, making the pilot work harder to reap benefits from the lift available.

Can a thermal be seen? The rising air itself is invisible, but it may be carrying dust, smoke or particles of debris. It may also be supporting soaring birds, such as hawks or vultures, or gliders. Some, but not all thermals are capped by a cumulus cloud in its early formative stages. Typically such clouds have a flat bottom and a smooth rounded top. Caution: Avoid being carried up into such a cloud. Cloud soaring is not only illegal in the United States and other countries, but potentially very dangerous. Within the cloud, the thermal's energy may be increased many times by the release of heat from condensation of vapor. A sailplane's rate of climb or descent in such a cloud could easily change by several thousand feet per minute.

Ordinarily the velocity in a clear air thermal ranges from just enough to neutralize sink (about 2½ feet per second) to three or four hundred feet per minute at altitudes between 500 and 8,000 feet above the ground. At the top of the thermal the air has cooled to that of the surrounding air. The cooler air sinks to replace that which was heated and lifted as a thermal. This sink rate is appreciably less than the updraft rate, since the air is dissipated over a wide area; however, the sink rate is fastest nearest the thermal. A low pressure area near the base draws air into the rising column or bubble from all directions. If windsocks could be planted around the perimeter of a thermal base, they would all blow in toward the center.

Thermals have another important characteristic. They usually lean. Although the base remains "attached" to the earth, the thermal bubbles drift as they rise, and they drift with the prevailing wind. The pilot who does not take this movement into consideration may lose his lift long before the updraft subsides.

The thermal hunter often senses an updraft first through "the seat of his pants," although, of course, his variometer or climb/descent instrumentation will confirm his impression with scientific accuracy. Beginning sailplane pilots are usually taught to roll into a gentle bank the moment they encounter lift and then fly three-quarters of a circle, noting which segment has the greatest lift. They try to circle toward the "core" of the thermal and endeavor to remain within the strongest lift area by flying in a continuous shallow or steep turn, as necessary, until they run out of lift or approach a cloud base overhead.

CLOUDS

Clouds tell a story to the soaring pilot who knows how to read them. Very often, they lead him to a thermal, but they may also reveal other power.

Large, white, billowing, puff-ball clouds, called cumulus clouds are dead giveaways for thermals. The clouds are formed when warm, moisture-laden air cools as it expands while ascending, and the moisture condenses into droplets of water. Beneath these clouds are fast-rising upcurrents of air. Seeking the power in and beneath these clouds is one of soaring's greatest thrills.

Other formations, such as wave clouds, also have something to offer the soaring pilot.

The soaring novice will find a totally new and fascinating world in meteorology. Its variety and complexity will surprise him. The more experienced soaring pilots much enhance their soaring proficiency by thorough side study and investigation of meteorology.

USING NATURE TO ADVANTAGE

Soaring pilots not only use the variometer to locate thermals, they also use Nature's external indicators. They watch for leaves rustling, which can sometimes be seen because from the air, the backs of leaves appear a lighter color. Also, grain or tall grass waving in a cultivated field is often an indication that a thermal may be coming up nearby. Small dust devils, too, tell wind direction and something of the lift to expect.

The sunny side of hills and ridges are good thermal sources. Any terrain that catches the direct rays of the sun is likely to generate some lift. Birds can be a help in locating lift, if they are circling. Don't assume that all birds are brilliant. They do sometimes circle when sinking! Most pilots agree, however, that if their sailplane is losing altitude and they are desperate for lift, going towards a circling hawk or a buzzard is a very good gamble. Remember, however, that the birds can circle in a much smaller thermal than a sailplane, hence it may not be possible to stay with them.

Soaring birds, such as hawks and turkey buzzards, have about the same sink rate and glide ratio at about 50 miles per hour as either an SGS 1-23 or maybe an SGS 1-26. They are, of course, more cleverly maneuverable and may be able to out-climb a sailplane. Most birds will not usually attack a sailplane, unless it is close to their nest or infringes deeply into their territory.

The pilots also watch for smoke. It indicates the direction of the wind, acting much like an airport wind sock. Smoke can also give some indication of the speed of the wind that is carrying it. Smoke that does not rise quickly or descend immediately to the ground indicates that local thermal conditions are poor. Smoke rises from embers or from a live fire and is carried upward by the heat from such sources. This heat helps the same way in developing a thermal as does ground heat in producing Nature's thermals. Smoke, especially that issuing from a prairie fire, or industrial smokestacks, suggests thermaling activity.

Like fishermen who have favorite haunts, soaring pilots have favored areas in the sky above certain parts of the land. Some pilots sweep over a plowed field or a stone quarry to see if a thermal is rising. Others prefer ridges bordering stretches of sandy beach. Once pilots get to know the thermal conditions over a particular piece of ground, they usually return to it when the weather is favorable for thermal activity at such a site.

There are certain "Blue Ribbon" days, of course, when no matter where the sailplane heads, there is plenty of lift! Soaring on such days is all sheer delight! If one could but get the necessary clearance for it,he could on such a day easily fly cross-country several hundred miles, or so he would feel. The main trouble, of course, is that those days just don't come often enough. In certain parts of the country, where from a soaring standpoint the topography could be a whole lot more desirable, such days may be encountered only once or twice during a whole summer. The weather factors making for such ideal days are often too difficult for the average soaring fan to forecast. But if one is fortunate enough to be aloft on such a day, he will really get to experience the thrill of soaring under the most ideal conditions!

MAPS AND NAVIGATION

Some students may be concerned about how to find their way about in the sky. This should really be no problem in the beginning stages of learning the sport, however, since the instructor will be in the cockpit to give directions if necessary. More than likely, most of the early instruction will be conducted close enough to the soaring center so that it will be visible virtually at all times while the student is aloft.

It will be primarily after the new pilot starts flying solo

that some knowledge of navigation will be necessary. Many of the essentials will have been learned in the ground instruction phases, and they will be augmented through practical flying navigation as the student gets into his instructional flights.

An understanding of navigation becomes very important when the pilot gets the urge to start ranging out from the glider port to go thermal hopping or when, perhaps, he gets a long tow from the takeoff strip to some well-known hill for a ride on the slope winds. It may be that getting back may take some navigational skill. Of course, the time when a pilot must have a keen knowledge of aerial navigation comes when he seeks the high-altitude wave, rides the currents through the mountains, or goes on a cross-country jaunt.

Before a student pilot can fly solo outside of a local area designated to him by his flight instructor, he must have received flight instruction from a certificated flight instructor in cross-country navigation. He will have had to use aeronautical charts and the compass and demonstrated his knowledge and ability to handle them to the instructor. At that point the instructor will endorse his student pilot certificate to the effect that the student is qualified to make cross-country flights.

While to most newly introduced to the sport there is no need to learn a lot about maps and navigation, nonetheless it is a good idea to become familiar with both, especially maps—in the beginning—since navigation in a sailplane relies heavily on maps (a power pilot also uses radio for navigation).

Aeronautical maps are adapted to the needs of a pilot just as road maps are designed to help a motorist find his way between two cities on the ground. There are no aeronautical maps especially made for soaring pilots. Most of them use what is commonly called the "sectional chart," a 1:500,000 map compiled by the Coast and Geodetic Survey of the U.S. Department of Commerce. One inch on such a chart equals 500,000 inches or approximately 8 miles on the ground. All nations have quite similar aeronautical charts, which are used by soaring pilots. The Australians use a 1:250,000 chart, where one inch is 4 miles on the ground.

Whether yet qualified for solo cross-country hops or not, it pays to study an aeronautical sectional chart. It contains an immense amount of information. If the instructor does not have one handy, possibly one may be borrowed from the tow plane pilot.

It is not the purpose of this book to go into the details of map reading and navigation, however, the beginning student can pick up much fundamental information by studying the wealth of information contained on a sectional map.

Roads, railroads and rivers will be easily recognized as such. The transparent blue lines that criss-cross hapazardly over the face of the chart are radio beams used only in radio navigation. Many of the puzzling, hieroglyphic-like symbols will become meaningful only when related to symbols on the back of the sectional. Along the lower edge of each chart are graphic scales in kilometers, nautical miles and conventional miles, which facilitate determining distance on the ground from distances on the chart.

Charts of this scale will likely not show much detail of the ground around the soaring site; hence, if the instructor has no objection, it would be wise to take one of these sectionals up on a flight and make some comparisons between what is shown on the chart versus that visible on the ground. This is a good way to get used to the chart and to learn a lot about reading it and how it depicts the ground below.

It will be difficult to really get much practical map reading experience while flying in the sailplane even under the best of conditions. It is not easy to unfold a chart to its full length—or even sometimes as needed to refer to a pre-drawn course—in the usually restricted space of a pilot's compartment. Moreover, especially if flying solo, the sailplane demands a lot of attention, and there is little time to study both map and ground and make comparisons of terrain and detailed landmarks.

Thus, if some cross-country soaring flying should be in the offing, try to get in a number of preliminary cross-country hops in a light airplane. Perhaps one with the tow pilot can be arranged when he takes a trip to another airport or some distant city. Learn what his route will be before each flight and watch him as he plots it. Try to duplicate this on a chart. When in the air, look for railroad tracks or other checkpoints which the course will cross, also rivers. Try to identify the small towns the plane passes over. Check such information with the pilot and don't hesitate to ask him for some help, particularly if the flight is smooth and easy, and the pilot has the time. Once a plane has reached cruising altitude the pilot will usually be looking for conversation, anyway, and be happy to help.

chapter 8

Learning Through Crewing

CREWING IS ONE part of the sport of soaring in which anyone can participate without extensive training. Going on a crewing jaunt is one of the best, no-cost ways of learning about the sport without ever leaving the ground. Meanwhile, it provides a lot of fun in the bargain.

There are several kinds of "crewing." Actually, the word comes from "ground crew." Ground crews are volunteers from clubs, or the paid crews of a commercial soaring school who help owners assemble sailplanes, handle the sailplanes from the hangar to the flight line, hitch the tow line, run with the wing, or stand at the edge of the strip, giving the signal for takeoffs.

But true crewing in soaring has a special connotation and is a very different and challenging operation. The real job of crewing involves driving an automobile, with an empty sailplane trailer in tow, to follow the flight of a sailplane in cross-country flight. The crew must be prepared to drive from five to five hundred miles and find where the sailplane has landed, there to assist the pilot disassemble it and make the long drive home. Or, the crew meets the pilot to take him to an airfield and help him prepare for the next leg of his journey. This is nothing like crewing in any other sport except, perhaps, kayaking.

"MAKING" THE CREW

A crew for this sort of task ideally consists of two or more people, and their equipment includes a car, a sailplane trailer, and a two-way radio capable of using the same frequencies as the sailplane's. A lot of crews are much more than this, and frequently a lot less as to the number of members and the kind of equipment they take along.

Sometimes a sailplane pilot may be able to persuade (or more likely, "draft") only his wife to the task. Many crewing operations also do not employ radio. As a matter of fact, most crews are just made up of families out for a weekend of fun. Others are volunteers from the club or they may be just some willing hands who have become known to the more active members at the site. Some clubs run rosters designating which of their members must stand by to supply or perform the crewing on a certain weekend or participate in crewing operations in support of a soaring contest.

A GOOD CREWMAN IS...

A good crewman has been humorously described as outgoing, generous, bubbling with energy, cheerful, obedient, intelligent, resourceful, unflappable, mechanically gifted, persistent, strong and healthy, crafty, intuitive—and possessing a way with highway patrolmen!

Barbed wire must not dismay him, nor fear of wild bulls nor surly farmers! He must be able to back a car and a 30-foot trailer through rush hour downtown traffic like a teamster. He should also know a little about operating a radio and even have some ability to repair it should it suddenly conk out. And, if no amount of kicking the radio or swearing at it will make it work, then he must be able to resort to his sixth sense or some prearranged telephone system in making rendezvous with the pilot.

METHODS OF OPERATION

Crewing groups are used basically in two different ways. They go out to retrieve a sailplane that ran out of lift and couldn't make it back to the local landing strip, or they go on a cross-country retrieval mission. In the first case the pilot probably has landed in some farmer's field not too far away from the takeoff site and someone, probably the pilot, has called the field, giving his location.

With the receipt of this message there is usually some flap and flutter around the operations center of the club or school, several individuals already briefed on crewing, hurriedly scanning a map to pinpoint the location of the downed sailplane, hopping into the car with an attached trailer and speeding off to the pilot's aid.

Or, the crewing job can turn into one of acting as a kind

of travelling, cross-country, ground operations center. This sort of crewing calls for a lot more expertise. Planning and coordination between the pilot and crew beforehand are important for this, too.

When a pilot plans a cross-country effort, he must prepare for two eventualities. The first is that he will reach his objective airport successfully and according to plan. Then, when he has landed there, he must arrange to get back to his own field. As to this, he has several choices. He can buy several hours of tow plane time and be towed home by air—a fairly expensive proposition, at times. As an alternative, he can pay for a tow to a desirable altitude, release, and then hopefully find enough lift to make his way back to his home field. Or, he can be met by his crew and trailer, who will help dismantle the sailplane, load it, and all return home.

Another eventuality—or contingency—is that somewhere en route to his objective, his lift may give out, and he will have to put down in a remote field. Then the crew comes in handy. If the pilot and his ground crew have two-way radio, so much the better. They can stay in constant voice contact, and before the pilot has to make his landing, he may even be able to direct his crew from the air and give them some idea of which road to take to get to where he will be waiting.

GETTING INVOLVED IN CREWING

The best way to become a good crew member is to know as much as possible about soaring through study and observation, for when crewing, it is important to know about thermals, clouds, flight operations, taking a sailplane apart, soaring locations and a host of other matters. But even the information in this little book combined with a little practical experience should be enough to start a newcomer on the road to becoming a crewing professional. The next step is to visit a soaring site. The tyro crewman should seek a pilot planning a cross-country flight and ask him if he needs a crew member. The pilot will probably want to know if the newcomer has dismantled a sailplane or crewed before. The newcomer should be able to tell him he has studied some and now wants some practical experience. There's a fair chance the pilot will put him on his team.

Meanwhile, until the crewing day arrives, the tyro should lend a hand in actual sailplane assembly and disassembly operations at the site. Only in this way can he get first-hand knowledge of how sailplanes come apart and how to handle the components so that they are not damaged. He should try to find opportunities to participate in local retrievals, if possible. This is good experience for the cross-country operations ahead.

PURSUING THE SAILPLANE

When a new man is asked to crew on a cross-country flight, he should be prepared. What and how well to prepare will depend on the nature and length of the proposed flight. He should take along a thermos of coffee or some cans of soft drinks and a sandwich. If it is inconvenient to take a sandwich, he should manage to tuck a few chocolate bars into a pocket. Crewing can be all-absorbing, and crews tend to forget about eating in their endeavors to keep the sailplane in sight or within radio contact. Bringing along a good pair of binoculars if available, is also a good idea.

Crews sometimes may barrel along at high speeds for

hundreds of miles on freeways and at other times they may have to sit and wait for hours, the sailplane maneuvering lazily overhead, getting just enough lift to keep at a safe altitude but not enough to be able to move on to another thermal. Crews should be prepared for either situation, or any number of others. Sailplanes have landed in swamps, in ten-foot snow drifts and out in the desert miles away from any distinguishable road.

Next a crew member should be certain to have some cash for emergencies. This is especially important in the case of crewing chiefs or drivers. Sailplane pilots sometimes become so absorbed in plans for their flight that they forget about some of these sordid little details, and it is well to prepare for any emergency. Sailplanes don't use gas on these cross-country jaunts, but automobiles do. It is surprising how much gas a car will need if it is hauling a 40-foot trailer.

To really be professional about crewing, a crewman should buy a piece of red bunting and make a flag for use in traffic. It will prove mighty useful when it becomes necessary to back up a trailer in a crowded street, for instance, just after making a telephone call from some service station. One or several flags can be used in many different ways to make the operation safer.

If it is at all possible, a new man should try to get some practice with the car and trailer that will actually be used before going out on a crewing operation. Driving with a sailplane trailer is something quite different than ordinary driving without any trailer at all. A sailplane trailer is long and lean; it handles quite different from a standard U-Haul or comparable auto trailer.

The best way to get some practice is to try it under the

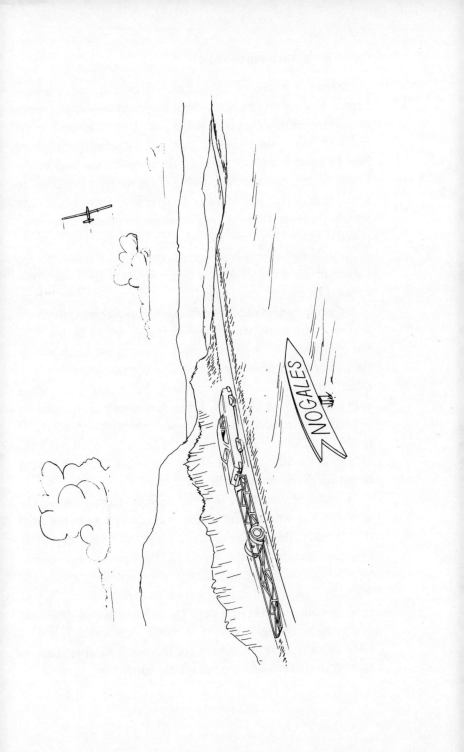

guidance of someone who has driven the combination before. Pulling any trailer at high speeds takes a high degree of driving skill and good judgment. New crewmen must learn to drive the trailer in tight traffic conditions, learn how to back it up and park it. They should not depend on previous driving expertise. Some clubs wisely have crewing practice sessions, particularly on overcast weekends during which they go through dry runs with equipment. They practice trailer backing and parking, sailplane disassembly, driving along narrow roads or over roadless terrain. A tyro crewman must try to get involved in one of these sessions, or see if he can get one started.

All crewmen should check on certain things, such as finding out exactly what car and trailer are to be used for the operation plus making certain that the car hitch will fit the trailer hitch. If car or trailer have been designed for each other, there should be no problem; but many times when club equipment is being used, the automobile and trailer do not have compatible hitches. A check should particularly be made to see that the front of the trailer, when hitched to the car, is not riding too low. If it is, there is danger that it might catch the ground while going over bumps.

In addition, scarcely any two trailers seem to have the same hookup attachments for lights, and lights are required in all states. Be certain that the auto and trailer electrical systems operate when connected. Because of its unusual length, an unlighted sailplane trailer speeding down the highway would be a special traffic hazard at night. One of the crew should take the auto trunk keys just in case it is necessary to change a tire. If the trailer has locks, it is wise to be certain to have the keys for them, too, and make sure that all spare tires are in good usable condition.

Check on the car-trailer combination by driving at different speeds to see if there is any instability or braking problem. Some sailplane trailers exhibit peculiar braking behavior.

If a radio is to be used, it should be pretested. Test conversations with the pilot before takeoff are essential. Whoever has to operate the radio should know every dial and switch and the purpose of each. Each pilot also has his own radio-use idiosyncrasies. Learn what they are for the pilot involved and try to get used to them ahead of time.

Radios are not always available, however. If no radio is to be used, the crew should have some other prearranged communication plan worked out, especially one for emergency or in case a radio conks out. This can often be set up by telephoning the home field, which relays the message somewhere else telling where the other party is. One pilot uses this arrangement with his wife, for instance. If she loses sight of his sailplane or otherwise loses track of it, she will call home where the baby sitter is with the children to see if her husband has called and left a message.

A crew also must have a good pre-flight planning conference with the pilot. A number of potential problems can then be discussed and taken care of at this time. The ground crew should have a copy of the same air navigation maps the pilot will carry plus a good state road map or maps, depending on how many states the pilot hopes to fly over during his cross-country.

A ground crew must become familiar with the approximate course the pilot will endeavor to follow and then pick out the major road networks along this course. Remember, when hauling a trailer it is best to stay on highways where it is possible to pull off the road to get oriented or take a squint into the sun to find the sailplane. There will be times, of course, when it is absolutely necessary to travel on narrow, unpaved, poor roads and in this area, county road maps may be helpful.

A crew should get a clear statement from the pilot on just what he expects to do if radio contact is lost. He may suggest leap frogging from gas station to gas station, using some nationally advertised gasoline chain that has its station locations marked on a road map. Perhaps the pilot will want his crew to call in every half hour to some specific telephone number during the forenoon, and to some other number farther along the course later in the day. He, of course, will agree to call the appropriate number when he lands.

Telephone Tips That Save Money

Here are some tips about telephone procedures which may save some money. Have a designated telephone manned, either at someone's home or at the soaring site. After the flight has started, and when there is a need to get an idea as to how things are progressing, the crew member makes a person-to-person call to that number, asking for the pilot by name. This is the cue to the person manning the phone that the call has to do with the crewing operation. If the pilot has not been heard from and there is nothing new, the person at the designated phone will refuse the call, and there is no charge. If the pilot has called in, then the call will be accepted and the necessary instructions and information given. Remember, when calling in, have the map, a pad and a pencil right at hand. Be specific about the questions asked at that time. Get the exact location of the sailplane, the

There are so many variables in cross-country soaring that ground crews can easily be left miles behind!

exact name of the motel or wherever the pilot may be—the name of the farmer whose property he is on,—and above all, the telephone number where the pilot can now be reached.

Making the Retrieval

By the time the crew has arrived, the pilot probably will have had the chance for reconnaissance and will be on or near a road within sight of the approaching crew to give directions, or lead them to the sailplane. At this point remember and follow these few listed courtesies; they will go a long way towards retaining and building good will for the sport of soaring:

- Always close the farmer's gate(s) in going from field to field

- Never climb over a wire fence

- Never cut a fence (in Texas this is considered about as serious as rustling)

- Stay out of fields where livestock are grazing

- Avoid driving or walking across cultivated fields

If lucky, a crew will be able to pull the trailer alongside the sailplane. Otherwise, it may mean hauling disassembled parts of the plane to where the trailer is parked. Remember the pointers on how to take a sailplane apart. Be especially careful when carrying major parts if the path back to the trailer is through thorny thickets or thick underbrush.

GOOD CREWMEN—INDISPENSABLE

Crewing presents many challenges and offers many rewards. It is in crewing that soaring, in the true sense, becomes a cooperative sport. No pilot who has had someone crew for him can overlook a good turn, nor will he.

When the time comes that a student can do his own flying, then it will be that he will cash in on some of the favors he has earlier done for other sailplane pilots as a member of their supporting crews. There is even some possiblity that these pilots may prove generous with the lending of their sailplanes to their former crewman.

A good crewman is where the pilot wants him, when he wants him, and is a person who is able to do what must be done, quickly, skillfully, and cheerfully. Newcomers to the sport who keep these things in mind will likely be asked to do a lot of crewing.

chapter 9

Additional Matters

AS THEY LEARN the sport, soaring enthusiasts will have many questions about what the future holds in terms of advanced soaring ratings, financial commitments, and other matters.

PRIVATE GLIDER PILOT CERTIFICATE

The Student Glider Pilot rating will enable the average soaring enthusiast to get all the soaring and about as much fun and challenge as he needs.

He is enabled to make local flights from any club, school,

or commercial glider soaring site and consistent with proficiency, to soar to his heart's content in that vicinity.

A percentage will become so enamored with the sport, that they will wish to take part in cross-country hops, high-altitude, and wave soaring. They will also want to qualify for advanced soaring badges. While some advanced soaring can be done while holding only the student rating, the cross-country soarer—the pilot who wants more independence—should apply for a Private Glider Pilot rating.

There are two major advantages to holding this level rating. The holder no longer needs to have his certificate recertified by an instructor every 90 days as required of the holder of a student rating. The private pilot rating revalidation is required only every two years. The holder may also make soaring flights without clearance by an instructor.

The enthusiastic soarer will find he can quickly build the necessary achievement for the private certificate. The major requirements are any of the following:

- 100 glider flights, including 25 during which a 360 degree turn was made or

- 10 hours of glider flight time, including 50 glider flights, or 30 glider flights using aero tows

- Three hours of instruction in light airplanes directed at glider training and seven hours of glider

flight time including 50 glider flights.

Moreover, the applicant has to show aeronautical skill by passing a test in preflight procedures and must show competence in preflight operations and ground launch systems. He also has to fly 180 degree approaches to landings, conforming to the prescribed traffic pattern flow and landing within 200 feet of a designated mark.

For the pilot already holding a private power rating, the requirements are less rigid. He must have at least two hours of glider flight time to include at least ten solo flights. He also is required to pass a flight test.

For the curious and those who wish to understand the level of experience of some of the soaring pilots with whom they associate, there are two other glider pilot certificates, "commercial" and "instructor." The former gives its holder the privilege to fly as a commercial pilot, that is as a pilot in charge of and responsible for his sailplare. He can carry passengers or property for compensation or hire.

The certified instructor rating allows the holder to teach soaring, endorse student certificates and carut other responsibilities. This takes an experienced person; for to qualify, he must first pass written tests on FAA regulations covering cross-country prodcedures.

THE SAILPLANE—TO BUY OR RENT

The question that will cross every soaring pilot's mind at some stage is whether or not to purchase a sailplane. The decision hinges on many considerations. Some have been discussed earlier. Perhaps the most important is the cost.

The choice of the right sailplane is most essential. A sailplane should have a high enough performance so that it can soar in average soaring weather. On the other hand, its flight characteristics should not be out of the range of the pilot's current handling ability, for a sailplane technically tuned beyond his ability presents an extra and unnecessary cost. The pilot wants to have fun soaring. He does not wish to have to devote most of his attention to handling a sailplane that is oversensitive. As his skills improve, and if he desires more performance, then he can swap or sell his sailplane for one with advanced characteristics. Also, a not-too-experienced student pilot or private pilot wants a craft he can use in cross-country flights, yet one he can land easily in small fields. It is tricky—to land a sailplane with a high glide ratio on a short landing strip.

NEW AND USED SAILPLANES

The U.S. has only one major sailplane manufacturer, although there are a number of smaller manufacturers all producing excellent models to suit a variety of tastes and needs. A growing number of sailplanes in the U.S. are high-performance European imports mainly from Germany, Czechoslovakia and Italy.

The prices of new sailplanes vary greatly. American models start at about $5,000. The Rolls Royce of sailplanes is a German-made, high-performance, 70-foot wingspan sailplane costing about $20,000.

Do not expect to find a secondhand sailplane at a bargain price while shopping. Sailplanes depreciate slowly. Occasionally, expect to find one of recent vintage selling for even more than its original price! This stems from the fact there is not enough U.S. production to keep up with swelling demand. It is possible, nevertheless, to buy a good used sailplane of fairly advanced design for from $4,000 to $7,000. *Soaring* advertises used sailplanes in each issue.

SGS 1-26

The most popular sailplane in the U.S. is Schweizer's SGS 1-26. The company has manufactured more than 550 of

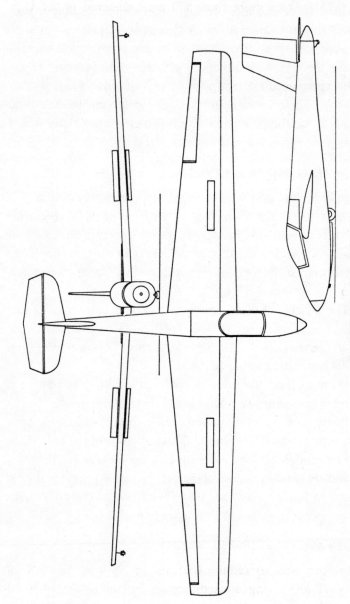

The SGS 1-26 sailplane.

these, of which more than 500 are registered in the U.S. alone.

This is a medium-size, single-place, sailplane. The fuselage is welded steel tubing. Wing parts are primarily of aluminum, but covered with fabric. The cockpit section is of welded steel tubing faired with a strong sheet metal skin. It gives the pilot ample room and protection. This sailplane has a 40-foot long wing, a 32.3-foot fuselage and it weighs about 575 pounds. Its sink rate is 2.7-feet per second, its glide ratio 23:1.

The SGS 1-26 handles easily, can be controlled at low speeds without trouble, and can land on very small fields. Two people can assemble or disassemble it with ease. It sells for $5,500. It is also available as a kit for considerably less.

SGS 2-33

This is a two-place trainer also produced by Schweizer and widely used in American soaring schools. Many pilots like to own it as a recreational sailplane since it allows the cooperative soaring of two pilots, or permits a member of the family or other passenger to take a pleasure ride. Made of metal with fabric over the fuselage and tail surfaces, it has a 51-foot wing, a 25.8-foot fuselage and weighs close to 600 pounds. Its sink rate is 2.8-feet per second and glide ration 23:1. It sells for $7,000.

KITS AND KIT BUILDING

Another way to reduce the cost of owning a sailplane, instead of buying a used one, is to build it from a kit.

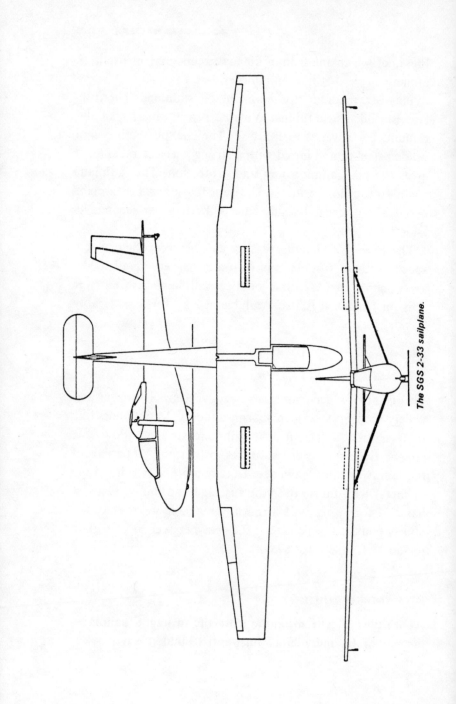

The SGS 2-33 sailplane.

Building a sailplane from a kit lowers costs by one-half to two-thirds of what it would cost to buy the same sailplane completely built by the manufacturer. Several manufacturers sell kits. The SGS 1-26 standard kit sells for $3,780 or about $2,000 less than the factory-built model, a sizable savings. Another manufacturer sells a kit for $2,500; another at $3,450.

The 1-26 comes in three different kits, "dry, standard, and uncovered and unfaired." The "dry" kit has the same basic parts as the "standard," but does not include the fabric and other finishing material, such as primer, wood sealer, thinner and the associated wood and plywood material.

The "standard" kit has all material and fabricated parts that are shown in the exploded view of the 1-26 in the accompanying illustration. The fuselage frame is already fabricated, the tubing welded and coated with olive-drab primer. The wings have already been aligned to the fuselage and all the difficult operations, including line-up work, has been done at the factory. This kit includes everything needed to make the ship ready to fly. The only extras that will be needed are instruments, a seat belt and shoulder harness.

The "uncovered" model is a structurally-complete sailplane with the exception that the job of covering the fuselage fairing, canopy and rear deck with fabric is left to the builder. Except for this, however, the sailplane is complete and ready for FAA inspection.

Tips to the Builder

The number of kits available from the different manufacturers gives the individual who wants to build his own sail-

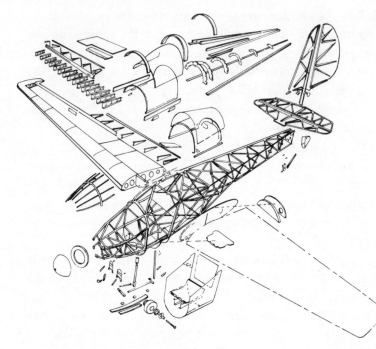

plane from kit up a considerable amount of latitude in se-
lecting one that fits his pocketbook and the amount of time
he can devote to its construction.

As a minimum, anyone expecting to build from a kit,
especially from one such as the dry kit of the SGS 1-26,
should plan to devote all his spare time to the task over a
four to six-month period. It is not unusual, in fact, to find
those who have worked as long as a year on the job of
building their sailplanes. In any case, it is not a quick "two-
or-three weekends" project.

Kits usually come crated with some crates measuring 21
X 3.4 X 5 feet. Most manufacturers ship them by truck to

the delivery point. A substantial shipping charge can be saved, however, by the purchaser if he goes to the factory with his own vehicle and trailer and hauls the crate home, himself.

Here are some thoughts that may save some heartaches for those intending to build their own sailplanes. The SSA has a list of suppliers of kits which it will furnish on request. Write to a number of these suppliers for information brochures about their product. Compare them. If possible, visit the plant where one of the sailplanes under consideration is made. Visit other manufacturers, too, if time permits. Each can show kits in the process of being manufactured. This will enable the purchaser to see for himself what he will be receiving in the large crate and understand what confronts him in building the sailplane. Ask to look at design plans and other materials sent with the kit. Get acquainted with the manufacturer's special brand of nomenclature and abbreviations. All this will save time and eliminate bewilderment and confusion in the construction process.

Also, be certain there is enough room to build the sailplane once it arrives. Remember, the fuselage alone will be close to 22-feet long, depending on the sailplane selected. Do not be like the individual who built a pleasure cruiser in his basement and found he could not get it through the door when it was completed. Most find the garage an ideal place to work in, since the average family garage is about 24-feet long, enough for housing the fuselage and yet permitting the garage door to be closed and locked.

Usually, no special jigs are needed for building the sailplane from the average kit. The hand tools found in the average home workshop suffice for much of the work that is to be done, although there are several special tools which will help ease certain of the operations. These are available from the kit manufacturer.

Once built, the sailplane must be certified by an FAA-liscensed inspector. Find out ahead of time where the inspector's office is located, and if possible, have a chat with him. The FAA's attitude towards a sailplane builder is naturally influenced by the attitude of the builder and the kind of work he does en route to the finished product. Tell the inspector what kit will be used and the site of the construction. He will have to inspect the sailplane at certain stages of construction. Stay in touch with him as the project moves along and thus avoid deferral or delay in ultimate certification stemming from lack of knowledge of some phase of the work or inspection concern about its quality.

It is advisable to get the FAA's *Aircraft Specification Sheet,* also known as a *Type Certificate Data Sheet.* This gives accurate and basic data for each aircraft manufactured. If one is not with the kit, it is wise to order it from the FAA. Then become thoroughly acquainted with the data sheet information on the sailplane.

The FAA agent who comes to inspect the completed sailplane will use this sheet in checking the sailplane at the time of certification. Suffice it to say, a little foreknowledge will go far to smooth the way in this more tedious, if informative, kit-building part of the sport.

Other inspection forms are in the kits. These are to be used as final check lists in making certain all required operations are accomplished to insure an airworthy sailplane. The specific operations are enumerated in the instruction manual; the inspection check list is used to check that the required operations are carried out correctly. There are provisions for signature by the builder and the FAA agent where operations require the agent's check before proceeding to next phase or final operations. These points should be predetermined with the agent who inspects the work at each step so that no cutting of the fabric or removing it from the fuselage, wing or tail surface is later required to check critical points.

Most important! The inspection forms as they are completed and signed should be *carefully* kept so that the complete set of inspection paperwork is available when presenting the sailplane for certification and flight test.

One of the best precautions is to purchase the FAA manual AC No. 4313-1, *Acceptable Methods, Techniques and Practices, Aircraft Inspection and Repair.* This handy volume is on sale by the Superintendent of Documents, U.S. Government Printing Office, Washington, D.C. 20402. In detail and purpose it goes far beyond the interests of the average kit constructor, but it has some valuable chapters and paragraphs that will save time and mistakes if read and followed. In addition, it is a good general reference book for maintenance and repair of light aircraft, such as a sailplane.

INSURANCE

The question of life insurance coverage on a soaring pilot arises sooner or later. Each insurance company has its own concepts with respect to a policyholder flying as a passenger or pilot. It is recommended that those who hold life insurance policies and have a desire to take up soaring consult their insurance company. Determine if coverage is in effect during both the instructional and solo phases. In this way the potential soaring pilot can protect his survivors under his existing policy. The chances are that the existing policy will give the needed protection and need not be modified nor any extra premium be charged.

PARACHUTES

Parachutes are not required for pilots engaged in soaring except for certain specific competitions sponsored by the SSA. However, some owners keep a parachute in their sailplane at all times and harness up in it for every flight.

It is always wise for anyone preparing to wear chutes to take certain precautions. First, it is necessary to inspect the parachute thoroughly. Too often a parachute is looked at indifferently or even derisively by inexperienced pilots who are inclined to use the packed chute as a cushion, or even toss one to the side of the field before takeoff. The result is that weathering and mishandling may occasionally damage the chute.

If the outside of the pack containing the parachute looks clean and fairly new looking and has been recently inspected, then there should be no cause for concern. Actually, according to Federal regulations, no pilot of an aircraft certificated by the FAA may allow a parachute to be carried for emergency use in that aircraft unless it is an approved model and has been inspected according to regulations. If other than the chair parachute, it must have been packed by a certificated and appropriately rated parachute rigger within the previous 60 days. A pilot is flying illegally if he has a parachute on board for emergency use, which does not meet these requirements. Thus, it is the pilot's responsibility to make certain the regulations are met, not the chute or aircraft owner's.

Certification is shown on a folded card filed in a pocket of the pack. Even though everything is "officially" in order, there are some other things to do. Take a second to check the pins that pull out and release the chute once the handle is pulled. In most cases these are covered by a flap. Unbutton the flap. The pins should be firmly seated into the studs. The last and most important item—be certain where the ripcord handle is and how to pull it. Put a hand around it and imagine using it as if it were the real thing.

Also, try on the parachute for fit well before the flight. Do not be embarrassed to do so. The leg and chest straps should be pulled to fit tightly when standing. Then take it off until time for the flight. Do not let anyone use it for a ground cushion. Expect that when wearing the chute in the sailplane things will be a bit more cramped than usual. A parachute takes up its full share of space in the close interior of the cockpit.

If forced to jump, release the canopy and open it as far as it can be opened quickly, or better yet and if it is this type, jettison it. The idea is to be sure to have ample space to get out without getting hung up on any edge or corner of the fuselage. Once out, if the pilot can retain his presence of mind, he should watch the sailplane and not pull the ripcord handle until the plane is far enough away to preclude damage to the billowing chute or any injury.

Landing in a chute can be tricky unless the jumper is relaxed. It is best to absorb the landing impact by hitting the earth with knees slightly bent. Then, as the knees bend further on impact, try to roll forward or fall to the side to the hips. One way to get a good idea of how this is done is to

An artist concept of Harris Hill, projected new National Soaring Museum in right foreground.

watch the sky-diving competitions appearing with increasing frequency on television, or go attend one of these contests. Reading a good book on the subject from the library can help, too.

ELMIRA, HARRIS HILL AND MUSEUM

Those who live in the Eastern U.S. will find a trip to Elmira, New York, interesting and profitable in the knowledge it will give about soaring. There, Schweizer Aircraft Corporation has a soaring school and plant where it manufactures sailplanes.

As with any school, its staff is experienced and can answer the innumerable questions the newcomer to the sport will have.

Only ten minutes away is Harris Hill, world famous for its soaring lift. Named for Lieutenant Henry B. Harris, who discovered its enduring and strong slope winds, it is the site of national and international competitions. Rare is the day, even the misty ones, where the visitor will not find at least several to ten or more sailplanes winging effortlessly above its forested boundaries. Sailplanes constantly takeoff from the short blacktop strip along its crest.

Nearby in a red brick building is the temporary home of the National Soaring Museum, well worth a visit. Only recently built to house a collection that has been accumulated over the years, it will in time give way to a much larger museum complex now being planned. Next to the soaring field is a park with a playground and picnic area.

Elmira lies close to many lakes and vacation facilities that can be used in combination with visits to the soaring facilities to make a pleasant several days to weeks vacation for soaring enthusiasts and their families.

Glossary

Aileron—A hinged, movable panel that is set into or near the trailing edge of each wing. It extends towards the tip and usually is contoured to the wing. It is used to control the rolling movements of the sailplane.

Airfoil—A wing or other surface shaped to obtain a reaction on itself, such as lift or thrust, from the air through which it moves.

Airspeed—The speed, stated in miles or kilometers per hour, of the sailplane through the air.

Air speed indicator—Instrument that registers the speed through the air.

Altimeter—Instrument that registers the height of the sailplane above the ground or above sea level, depending on how it was set before takeoff.

Altitude—Height of the sailplane above the starting point or above sea level.

Angle of attack—Angle between the chord and the direction which the sailplane moves through the air in a vertical plane.

Angle of incidence—Angle between the chord and the longitudinal axis of the sailplane.

Aspect ratio—Ratio of the span of the wings from tip to tip to the average width of the wing (mean chord).

Attitude—Aspect, posture, position at any moment as determined by the inclination of a sailplane about its three axes.

Axis—Line in any of the longitudinal, (nose to tail) lateral, (wing tip to wing tip) or vertical planes that passes through the sailplane's center of gravity.

Bank—Attitude when lateral axis is inclined with respect to the horizontal. Also a roll about the longitudinal axis.

Biplane—Aircraft with two wings, one set above the other.

Center of gravity—Center of weight of a sailplane. If at rest on a sawhorse placed directly under this point, the sailplane would balance perfectly.

Central runner. Central skid—Ski-like object under fuselage upon which sailplane lands and rests while on the ground.

Chord—Width of a cross section of a wing measured from the leading edge of the cross section to the trailing edge.

Crab—Simultaneous sideward and forward movement through the air.

Control surface—Surfaces that control the rolling, pitching

or yawing of the sailplane. The ailerons, rudder, elevator.

Dihedral—Angle between horizontal line drawn laterally from center of bottom side of wing and line formed by wing inclined upwards.

Dive—Steep forward descent through the air.

Drag—A resistant force exerted in a direction opposite to the direction of flight. It comes from the wing, fuselage, and other parts of the sailplane pushing through the air.

Drift—Crabwise motion of sailplane, relative to the ground. Deviation in course caused by wind. Angle between sailplane's course and the direction its nose is pointed.

Dual control—Two complete sets of pilot controls so that either the pilot or the passenger can fly the sailplane without changing seats.

Elevator—Hinged, horizontal tail surface that forces sailplane to raise or lower the nose, i.e. change the angle of attack.

Empennage—Tail of the sailplane including all fixed and movable surfaces.

Fairing—Rigid material shaped to streamline a part of the sailplane so as to reduce drag. In a sense, the plastic canopy is fairing for the cockpit. While the canopy does serve other purposes, it does reduce the amount of drag which an open cockpit would otherwise induce by forcing the wind to go smoothly over or around the cockpit.

Fin—Fixed vertical tail surface to which rudder is hinged. Fin also gives sailplane longitudinal (yaw) stability.

Flaps—Movable panels hinged to rear of wings between the ailerons and fuselage. The pilot activates them to increase lift and drag. Only a few modern sailplanes feature flaps.

Flare (out)—Final approach procedure in landing as the pilot changes the attitude of the sailplane from a descending one to one that is parallel with the ground.

Fuselage—Body of the sailplane.

Glide—Literally coasting downhill in the air, gravity furnishing the motive power.

Glider—Winged, motorless aircraft that flies through the air in gradually descending flight, depending on gravity for power.

Glide ratio—Ratio of distance covered horizontally to height lost vertically. Also known as L/D.

Ground speed—Speed of the sailplane relative to the ground.

Landing speed—Speed at which sailplane touches the ground.

Leading edge—Front edge of a wing.

Lift—Upward component of force created by an airfoil as it moves through the air. Also, the available upward air currents.

Log—A detailed record of each flight made by a pilot or an instructor as required by the FAA.

Monoplane—Aircraft with a single supporting surface (wing).

Nacelle—An enclosed body, usually containing the cockpit, and shorter than the standard fuselage, but not including the empennage.

Pancake (to)—To drop to the earth from a few feet as a consequence of a loss of flying speed, which in turn usually results from flaring out too soon in landing.

Porpoising—Motion a sailplane makes on occasion during

takeoff or landing that resembles the motion of a por-poise through the water.

Release—The knob or device in the cockpit that the pilot activates to release the sailplane from the tow plane.

Red line—Red line or mark placed on the face of the air-speed indicator as the point of maximum speed which is safe for that sailplane.

Rollout—Path of sailplane from point of touchdown to point of halt.

Roundout—The point just short of release when the rate of climb is slowing and the sailplane is close to normal glide angle.

Rudder—Tail panel hinged to vertical fin for directional control in horizontal plane. It overcomes yaw.

Sailplane—Aircraft built for soaring flight.

Sink—An area in the atmosphere where there are descending currents of air, which cause the sailplane to lose altitude faster than in still air.

Soar—Fly without the power of an engine and without loss of altitude.

Sock—Wind indicator found at most airfields. A cloth cone, open at both ends and suspended from a pole to indicate wind direction.

Span—Distance from wing tip to wing tip.

Spin—Spinning rapidly downward, nose down, about one wing which is stalled.

Spoiler—Small panel which the pilot can raise vertically above the wing to disturb the flow of the air over the surface of the wing. This decreases the lift of the wing and accelerates the sailplane's descent.

Stability—Ability or tendency of a sailplane to return to a

normal flying position if hands and feet are removed from the controls.

Stabilizer—Fixed, horizontal tail panel that gives stability in the vertical plane and dampens any tendency for the sailplane to pitch.

Stall—A dangerous condition of the sailplane in the air when there is insufficient or no lift to support the sailplane. It results from insufficient air speed over the wing and is corrected by putting the nose down to regain suitable flying speed.

Strut—A bar or rod used as a brace or stress member in the structure of the sailplane, such as a wing strut.

Stick—Control within the cockpit used to move the ailerons and elevator.

Tail skid—Skid at bottom of the tail of the sailplane to support the tail when the sailplane is in contact with the ground.

Takeoff—The start of a flight.

Towline—Rope, cable or wire used to tow a sailplane.

Trailing edge—Rear edge of a wing or other airfoil.

Upcurrents—Rising currents of air.

Wake—The turbulent air behind an aircraft.

Wing—Supporting surface of a sailplane.

Wing loading—Weight of a sailplane fully loaded divided by the area of the main wing.

Yaw—Turn flatly from side to side about the vertical axis.

Abbreviations

SSA—Soaring Society of America
FAA—Federal Aviation Administration
AGL—Above ground level
IAS—Indicated airspeed
TAS—True airspeed
FAI—Federation Aeornautiqué Internationale
L/D—Lift over drag
G—Gravity

Characteristics of Seven Well-Known Sailplanes

	Schweizer (United States)			Omnipol Ltd. (Czechoslovakia)	Glasflugel (Germany)	Slingsby (United Kingdom)	Schempp-Hirth (Germany)
	SGS 1-26	SGS 1-34	SGS 2-33	Blanik	Libelle (Standard)	Kestrel 19	Nimbus
Specifications							
Wingspan (feet)	40	49.2	51	53	49.2	62.3	72.4
Wing area (square feet)	160	151	219.5	206	106	138.5	
Aspect ratio	10	16	18	13.7	23	28	
Weights (pounds):							
Empty	420	570	600	644	407	699	825
With load	575	800	1040	1102	610	1,040	1050
Payload	220	250	440	458	203	341	225
Wingloading (pounds per square foot)	3.59	5.3	5	5.35	6.07	6.35	
Performance							
Glide ratio (L/D) (e.g. 23:1 @ 49 mph)	23@49	34@55	23@45	28@58	38@53	44@60	50@48
Minimum sink (feet per second)	2.7@40	2.1@47	2.8@40	2.7@40	1.8@47	1.7@46	1.5@56
Maximum speed (mph)	160	135	98		237	121	160
Stall speed (mph)	32		31 (solo)		39	37	39
Price (approximate U.S. dollars)	5,500	8,000	7,000	6,500	5,800		12,000

Some American Soaring Centers

(Instruction usually available.)

WESTERN

Wave Flights, Inc.
9990 Gliderport Rd., Colo. Springs, Colo. 80908. Ph: 303 495-4144

Arizona Soaring, Inc.
Box 427, Tempe, Ariz. 85281
Ph: 602 568-2318

Great Western Soaring School
Box 148, Pearblossom, Cal. 93533
Ph: 805 944-2920

Holiday Soaring School
Box 16, Tehachapi, Cal. 93561
Ph: 805 822-3736

Sky Sailing Airport
44999 Christy, Fremont, Cal. 94538
Ph: 415 656-9900

Eagle Flight Center
Portland Hillsboro Airport, Hillsboro, Ore. 97123. Ph: 503 648-7151

Soaring Unlimited, Inc.
Skyport (Arpt), Issaquah, Wa. 98027
Ph: 206 454-2514

CENTRAL

West Bend Flying Service
Box 409, West Bend (Arpt), Wis. 53095. Ph: 414 334-5603

Southwest Soaring Enterprises
Box 175, Rockwall, Texas 75087
Ph: 214 722-8819

Texas Soaring Center
Box 1271, San Marcos, Tex. 78666
Ph: 512 392-9293; 392-3133

C. C. Holt, Box 12248
Houston, Tex. 77017
Ph: 713 944-8562

EASTERN

Sugarbush Soaring
Warren (Arpt), Vt. 05673
Ph: 802-496-2290

Northeastern Light Aircraft
Box 425, Methuen, Mass. 01844
Ph: 617 688-6019

Wurtsboro School of Aviation
Wurtsboro (Arpt), N.Y. 12790
Ph: 914 888-2791

Hudson Valley Aircraft, Box 296
Randall Fld., Middletown, N.Y.
10940
Ph: 914 343-8883

Kutztown Aviation Services
Kutztown (Arpt), Pa. 19530
Ph: 215 683-3821

Capital Area Soaring School
Warrenton (Airpark), Va. 22186
Ph: 301 559-5140

Strawberry Hill Soaring Center
Box 98, Advance, N.C. 27006
Ph: 919 998-4504

Bermuda High Soaring School
Box 134, Chester (Arpt), S.C.
29706
Ph: 803 385-6061; 385-5764

Antique Acres Airstrip
Williamson, Ga. 30292
Ph: 404 277-8282

Chase-Air, Plantation Airpark
Sylvania, Ga. 30467
Ph: 912 857-3220

Lenox Flight School
Rt. 1, Box 170, Mulberry
Fla. 33860 Ph: 813 425-1352

Aero Sport, Inc.
Box 1615, St. Augustine,
Fla. 32084 Ph: 904 829-1995

Cardinal Aviation
Columbiana Arpt., E. Liverpool,
Ohio 43920. Ph: 216 386-3761

Northern Ohio Soaring
Jefferson (Arpt), Ohio 44047
Ph: 216 576-4896

Soaring Society of Dayton
Box 581, Dayton, Ohio 45419
Ph: 513 299-1943

Schweizer Soaring School
Box 147, Elmira, N.Y. 14902
Ph: 607 739-3821